SELECT BIBLIOGRAPHY
for the study of
ANGLO·IRISH
LITERATURE
and its backgrounds

AN IRISH STUDIES HANDBOOK

Maurice Harmon

WOLFHOUND PRESS

First published 1977

© 1977 Maurice Harmon
Maps © 1977 Wolfhound Press

ISBN 0 905473 04 3
ISBN 0 905473 05 1

Wolfhound Press, publishers
98 Ardilaun Portmarnock County Dublin

828.99(016)

Select Bibliography for the Study of Anglo-Irish
Literature and its Backgrounds

AN IRISH STUDIES HANDBOOK

By the same Author

Sean O'Faolain: a critical introduction. University of Notre Dame Press (Notre Dame & London, 1967).

Modern Irish Literature, 1800-1967: a reader's guide. Dolmen and OUP (1967). Dufour, Pa. (1968).

Fenians and Fenianism: centenary essays. Ed. Scepter (Dublin, 1968). University of Washington (Seattle, 1969).

The Celtic Master: Being contributions to the first James Joyce Symposium in Dublin. Ed. Dolmen and OUP (1969). Dufour Pa. (1970).

J. M. Synge centenary papers 1971. Ed. Dolmen and OUP (1972). Humanities Press (New York, 1972).

Malone Shakespeare: King Richard II, Romeo and Juliet, King Lear, Coriolanus. Ed. Longman, Brown and Nolan (1970-72).

William Carleton. *Wildgoose Lodge and other stories; Denis O'Shaughnessy going to Maynooth; Phelim O'Toole's Courtship and other stories; The Party Fight and Funeral.* 4 vols., ed. Mercier Press (Cork & Dublin, 1973),

The Poetry of Thomas Kinsella: 'With darkness for a nest'. Wolfhound Press (Dublin, 1974). Humanities Press (New York, 1975).

The Irish novel on our time. Ed. with P. Rafroidi. (Lille, 1976).

Contents

ANGLO-IRISH LITERATURE

CHRONOLOGY

MAPS

Acknowledgements

One of the pleasures in preparing this book came from discussions with scholars in the various disciplines it embraces. I am grateful to all those who gave help and encouragement, particularly to Michael Herity, Tomás de Bhalraithe, Proinsias MacCana, Donal McCartney, Tomás Ó Concheanainn, Kevin Danaher, Seán Ó Súilleabháin, Alan Bliss and Roger McHugh. I also had the benefit of advice from a number of librarians — Mairin Cassidy, Mary Pollard, Alan Eager and particularly from Alf MacLochlainn who helped to give the book its final shape. When Malcolm Brown arrived in Dublin I could not resist the opportunity to avail of his expert advice. Finally, I am specially grateful to Margaret MacAnulla of the Royal Irish Academy for her generous help and encouragement.

I am also pleased to acknowledge a grant towards the publication of this book from the National University of Ireland.

Introduction

The emergence of a distinctive literature in Ireland has been
one of the major literary developments of the late nineteenth
and early twentieth centuries. Before the Irish Literary
Revival ended, Irish writers had produced major works in
each genre and the whole course of modern literature had
been affected by the achievements of W.B. Yeats and James
Joyce. Nor was the Revival a momentary phenomenon.
In the last fifty years, in the work of Sean O'Casey, Flann
O'Brien and Samuel Beckett, the ideas and directions first
created by Yeats and his contemporaries were applied, developed and redirected to suit the needs and aspirations of
successive generations of writers.

Central to the tradition is the fact that the literature draws
upon two separate cultures, the Irish and the English, and
that these interact one upon the other. The degree and
the nature of that interaction vary from time to time and
from one writer to the next, but the dual heritage is perhaps
the most important single factor in the literature as a whole.

Irish literary studies reflect this duality. The various professional organisations are interdisciplinary in their membership
and in their subject-matter; in the universities in Ireland
and elsewhere the study of Anglo-Irish literature increasingly

involves the study of its contexts as well. In such matters our inquiry is dictated by the writers. If they find it necessary and valuable to draw upon mythology, folklore, history, Gaelic literature and so on, we have no alternative but to follow in their footsteps. That principle is fundamental to the development of a critical response that is adequate to the literature. Increasingly among Irish writers there is the impulse to explore and to understand the roots from which they have come and there is the habitual need to compensate for deficiencies within the heritage by drawing widely from outside cultures. Both of these lead to the production of a literature that draws deeply and widely from the whole spectrum of the Irish past and that ranges well beyond the shores of the island and beyond the confines of the two major traditions of the Irish and the English.

It is not easy for the student to cope with a literature that is so rooted in tradition and so widespread in its affinities. His difficulty is compounded by the lack of specific supporting reference, bibliographic and scholarly material. Even the criticism has been selective and sporadic. The purpose of this handbook is to bring some order into the study of the literature by listing the essential reference sources, the primary research materials and a bibliography of adequate background reading. Primary texts are not listed, since they are mentioned in the bibliographies. My other guide, *Modern Irish literature 1800-1967* (Dublin 1967) provides a listing of novels, poetry, plays and criticism.

The first section, 'Background: general reference' lists work which may also be found in comparable guides to English studies, such as Richard D. Altick and Andrew Wright, *Selective bibliography for the study of English and American literature* (1971); Donald F. Bond, *A Reference guide to English studies* (1971); Arthur G. Kennedy and Donald B. Sand, *A Concise bibliography for students of English* (1960), or F. W. Bateson, *A Guide to English literature*

(1967). Their more extensive coverage in this area complements the present guide and may be consulted by the student of Anglo-Irish literature. None are fully adequate to his particular needs. He must turn to those works of reference, to bibliographies, to literary histories, to periodicals and to other publications which deal specifically with his subject. He will find them listed in this guide.

The book is organised in a pattern from general to particular, from general background material, to background material specifically Irish, to the literature itself. Within these major divisions the running heads provide the control. Items throughout are listed in alphabetical order. Although the bibliograpies in each section are selective, they try to provide directions for further reading. The reader will note the existence of several specialist bibliographies, such as those by Best, Bromwich, Danaher and Eager, and those works in which there are comprehensive bibliographies.

Background: General Reference

Background: General Reference

Introduction

This section is divided into six parts:

Libraries	dissertations
bibliographies of bibliography	literature: books
biographies	literature: newspapers and periodicals

Its aim is to provide a list of major reference works which are useful for the student of Anglo-Irish literature. It cannot hope to be exhaustive, since virtually every reference aid to English studies, including those in some foreign languages, is likely to contain something of use to Anglo-Irish studies. It should therefore be noted that several guides to English studies are available; some have already been mentioned in the Introduction to this guide. They provide a more comprehensive coverage of general reference material than this specialist work. The student of Anglo-Irish literature will realise that the backgrounds and extensions to be found in English literature, such as those in European literature, classical literature or the bible, are also likely to be relevant to his study. There are, it is well to remember, dictionaries and encyclopaedias for virtually every subject; and there are directories, yearbooks, indexes, serial bibliographies and other reference material besides those listed in this guide.

The student should know his Altick and Wright or his Bateson. He should also know the standard aids to libraries, such as Constance M. Winchell, *Guide to reference books;* A. J. Walford, *Guide to reference material* and James Thompson, *English studies: a guide for librarians to the sources and their organisation.* There is no good reason to be unaware of books that professional librarians find invaluable.

Libraries

Printed catalogues of libraries are useful reference aids: they verify titles, give information about authorship, describe books, editions, contents and sometimes provide other useful notes. Naturally the catalogues of the great national libraries such as the British Museum, the Bibliothèque Nationale, the Library of Congress or the National Library of Ireland are of special importance, because these libraries receive copyright copies of all books published in their respective countries. Their catalogues are therefore the most comprehensive single records of publications in these countries.

ASLIB Directory: a guide to sources of specialised information in Great Britain and Ireland. (Association of Special Libraries and Information Bureaux). ed. Miriam Alman. 2 vols. London, 1957.
Supplement, 1960-61.

Vol. 1 shows which libraries specialise in certain subjects; vol. 2 is a directory of libraries arranged alphabetically by city.

British Museum. Department of Printed Books. **General catalogue of printed books.** vol. 1—. London, 1931 —. Photolithographic edition to 1955. 263 vols. London, 1959-66. Decennial Supplement 1956-65. 50 vols. London, 1968. Additions, 1963—. London, 1964. (Annual).

This complete record of the printed books in the library of the British Museum is an indispensable bibliographical and reference source.

———. Supplement: **Newspapers published in Great Britain and Ireland, 1801-1900.** London, 1905.

A valuable record of nineteenth-century newspapers. Newspapers prior to 1801 are listed in *Catalogue of printed books. . . periodical publications,* 2 vols., (1899-1900).

See also the British union catalogue of periodicals under 'Background: general reference: literature: newspapers and periodicals'.

Library of Congress. **A catalog of books represented by Library of Congress printed cards, issued to July 31, 1942.** 167 vols. Ann Arbor, Michigan, 1942-46.

Supplement: cards issued 1 Aug. 1942—31 Dec. 1947. 42 vols. Ann Arbor, 1948.

Continuation is provided by:

Library of Congress author catalog (1948-52).

National union catalog: 1952-55 imprints.

National union catalog: a cumulative author list (1953-57).

National union catalog: a cumulative author list. Washington, 1956 —.

These records are an invaluable bibliographical source. The information in the national union catalog is accurate, gives full name of author, dates of birth and death, full title, place, publisher and date of publication and other data.

Together with the *Cumulative book index* these catalogues form a comprehensive record of American publishing since 1898.

National Library of Ireland. **List of publications under the terms of the Industrial and Commercial Property (Protection) Act, 1927.** no. 1-5, August, 1927/December, 1929-1935/36. Stationery Office, Dublin, 1930-37.

Annual.

Contents: 1. Books and pamphlets; 2. Annuals; 3. Periodicals and publications of societies; 4. Official publications issued by the Stationery Office; 5. Newspapers; 6. Music; 7. Maps.

National Library of Ireland (continued).

This publication lapsed with World War II; following the enact-
ment of the 1963 Copyright Act similar lists compiled by the
National Library were published in *An Leabharlann* (1964-68).
The *Irish Publishing Record* (1967 —) covers the same field and
is a current national bibliography.

———. Reports of trustees. Dublin, 1877.

Trinity College Library, Dublin.
An authoritative article on this library appeared in the *Times
Literary Supplement*, 16 March 1956, p. 172. This long establish-
ed library also benefits under the copyright laws of England and
Ireland, although it is selective in what it accepts.

Bibliographies of Bibliography

These general indexes provide information on existing bibliographies in book-form and in periodicals. The student should develop the habit of checking them before he begins some line of reading or of research.

Besterman, Theodore. A World bibliography of bibliographies and of bibliographical catalogues, calendars, abstracts, digests, indexes and the like. 4th ed. 5 vols. Lausanne, 1965-6.
Very useful for bibliographies up to 1960.
Has separate categories for Ireland and for Irish language and literature.

Bibliographical index: a cumulative bibliography of bibliographies (1937 –), New York, 1938–.
Semi-annual, bound annual and 3-year cumulations.
Indexes current bibliographies by subject, including those published separately as books and pamphlets, and those appearing as parts of books, pamphlets and articles. Includes bibliographies in periodicals. The standard current bibliography of bibliographies.

Collison, Robert L. **Bibliographies subject and national: a guide to their contents, arrangement and use.** 3rd. ed. revised and enlarged. London, 1968.

Courtney, William P. **A Register of national bibliography.** 3 vols. London, 1905-12.

A standard work. Alphabetically by subjects with author index. Vols I-2: bibliographies published before 1905; vol. 3: those published 1905-12.
Includes bibliographies in periodicals.

Howard-Hill, T.H. **Index to British bibliography.** vol. 1: **Bibliographies of British literary bibliographies.** Oxford, 1969.

Good section on Ireland, pp. 101-12.

Biographies

The main sources for biographical sketches of authors of any country are the encyclopaedias and national biographies of the country. It has to be said, however, that while the standard biographical sources listed below are useful for many Irish writers, none are fully comprehensive in their coverage, nor as complete in their information as one would like. In the absence of an Irish dictionary of national biography we have to use these standard dictionaries of biographies and these indexes, but they have to be supplemented from other sources, some of which are to be found under 'Background: Ireland: biography'.

Allibone, S. Austin. **A Critical dictionary of English literature and British and American authors.** 3 vols. Philadelphia and London, 1858-71.
Supplement by J. F. Kirk. 2 vols, Philadelphia and London, 1891. (reprint, New York, 1965).

> Has information on thousands of writers. Its usefulness is too often underestimated.

MUNSTER

Adapted from *A Literary Map of Ireland*, compiled by Maurice Harmon and designed by Jarlath and Susan Hayes (Wolfhound Press, 1977).

CLARE

Desmond O'Grady
1935—— Limerick
Gerald Griffin
1803-1840 Limerick
Kate O'Brien
1897-1974 Limerick

George Fitzmaurice
1877-1963 Listowel
J.B. Keane
1928—— Listowel
Bryan MacMahon
1908—— Listowel
Brendan Kennelly
1936—— Ballylongford

Aubrey De Vere
1814-1902 Adare

LIN

Michael Hartnett
1941—— Newcastle West

M U N

Peig Sayers
1873-1958 Dunquin
Thomas O'Crohan
1856-1937 Blasket islands
Muiris O'Suilleabhain
1904-1950 Blasket islands

Thomas Davis
1814-1845 Ma

Aodhagan O'Rathaille
1670-c.1728 Killarney
Eoghan Ruadh O'Suilleabhain
1748-1784 Killarney

KERRY

Sean O'Riordain
1917-1977 Ballyvourney

T.C. Murray
1873-1959 Macroom

Diarmuid O'Suilleabhain
1932—— Eyeries Beara
Standish James O'Grady
1846-1928 Castletown Berehaven

Edith Somerville
1858-1949 Bantry (b.Corfu)
Martin Ross
1862-1951 Bantry (b. Co. Galway)

Thomas Mac Donogh
1878-1916 Cloughjordan
O'Brien
— Scarriff
Merriman
8 Feakle

TIPPERARY

Limerick City

Charles Kickham
1828-1882 Mullinahone

S T E R

th Bowen
73 Bowen's Court (b. Dublin)

iver Blackwater

WATERFORD

David O'Bruadair
c.1625-1698

er Lee   *Cork City*

CORK CITY

Jeremiah Joseph Callanan
1795-1829
Daniel Corkery
1878-1964
Patrick Galvin
1927——
Eilean Ní Chuilleanáin
1942——
Frank O'Connor
1903-1966
Sean O'Faolain
1900——
Sean O Tuama
1926——
Lennox Robinson
1886-1958

Biography index: a cumulative index to biographical material in books and magazines. New York, 1947 — .
Quarterly with bound annual and permanent 3-year cumulations. Vol. 1, 1946/49 —.

The standard biography index: very useful and comprehensive. Includes current English language books wherever published and biographical material from a wide range of periodicals.

Dictionary of national biography. eds. Leslie Stephen and Sidney Lee. 22 vols. reissue. London, 1908-9. (reprint, 1938).

Vols. 1-21, A-Z, Vol. 22, 1st supplement, additional names, 1901. 2nd-6th supplements, 5 vols., (Oxford, 1912-59).

————. **Index and epitome.** ed. Sidney Lee. 2 vols. London, 1903-13.

Contents: index and epitome to main set and 1st supplement, 22 vols, (2nd ed. 1906); index to 2nd supplement, (1913).

The DNB contains many Irish biographies. (See article in *Irish Book Lover* under section, 'Background: Ireland: biography'.) It is the most important reference work for English biography, containing signed articles by specialists, and excellent bibliographies.

————. **The Concise dictionary.** 2 vols. Oxford, 1903, (reprint, 1953-61).

Part 1, from the beginnings to 1900 is an epitome of the main work and its supplement. The 1953 reprint lists corrections and additions on pp. 1457-503, which in many cases correct or amplify the main work. Part 2, 1901-50 is an epitome of the twentieth century *Dictionary of national biography*. Includes a select subject index, pp. 485-528.
The Concise dictionary serves a double purpose, i.e., it is both an index and also an independent biographical dictionary, as it gives abstracts of the original articles.

Kunitz, Stanley J. and H. Haycraft. Twentieth century authors, a biographical dictionary of modern literature; complete in one volume with 1,850 biographies and 1,700 portraits, New York, 1942.
Supplement. Updated. New York, 1955.

Somewhat popular in approach but usefully comprehensive; also has bibliographies.

Matthews, William. **British autobiographies: an annotated bibliography of British autobiographies published or written before 1951.** Berkeley, 1955.

Arranged alphabetically by author, with index of professions and occupations.

Who was who, 1897-1960. 5 vols. London, 1920-61.

Useful, concise references; companion to the following entry.

Who's who: an annual biographical dictionary. London, 1849 –.

A standard reference work; biographical dictionary of prominent people in many fields.

Dissertations

Because of the widespread growth in the study of Anglo-Irish literature, there is an increasing number of theses being done in this area. Students doing advanced work should therefore find out what is being done or has been done in theses relevant to their own work.

Theses can be sometimes very helpful, specially those written under the direction of an authoritative and responsible director: they often contain excellent critical observations, sometimes explore important aspects of a particular topic and frequently their bibliographies of primary and secondary material are the most comprehensive in existence.

In addition to these general indexes, the student should consult the specialised listings published by the Royal Irish Academy. See under 'Anglo-Irish literature: general'.

ASLIB index to theses accepted for higher degrees in the universities of Great Britain and Ireland. vol. 1—., (1950/1—.) London, 1953—.

Published annually.

Comprehensive dissertation index Ann Arbor, Mich., (1861-1972. 37 vols. University Microfilms Ltd.

Subject and author index to doctoral dissertations.
Yearly supplements.

Dissertation abstracts international. Ann Arbor, Mich., 1935 —. Monthly.

Title 1935-51, *Microfilm abstracts;* 1951-69, *Dissertation abstracts.*

Since 1966 (vol. 27) it has been divided into two series: humanities and social sciences, and the sciences. It is a compilation of doctoral dissertations submitted to University Microfilms; the theses are microfilmed and can be bought from UM. An abstract for each is included in *Dissertation abstracts.* Each issue has subject and author index. Not included are those in the *Index to American doctoral dissertations.* See under *Doctoral dissertations* below.

Doctoral dissertations accepted by American universities, 1933/34 — 1954/55. 22 vols. New York, Wilson, 1934-1955.

Ceased publication. Covers United States and Canada.
Alphabetical author index and subject index.
Continued by *Index to American doctoral dissertations, 1955/56 —.*
The *Index* is issued annually as no 13 of *Dissertation abstracts.* It consolidates into one list dissertations for which doctoral degrees were awarded in North America in the academic year being dealt with, including those available on microfilm. Arranged by subject and with author index.

Literature: Books

It is often essential to know what books are currently in print or were available at a particular time in the past. The catalogues, indexes and serial bibliographies listed here refer to British, Irish and American imprints. They verify the existence of certain books or editions and may be used in conjunction with the great library catalogues and with national, general and specialist bibliographies. It is advisable to refer to items under both 'Background: general reference: literature: books' and 'Background: general reference: literature: newspapers and periodicals' since it is virtually impossible to separate the catalogues and other entries.

American book publishing record. New York, 1960 —.

Includes same information as *Publishers' Weekly,* cumulated monthly and rearranged by subject; indexed by author and title. Provides a complete record of American books published.

Of narrower scope but very useful are *Paperbound books in print* (New York, 1955 —), *Paperbacks in print* (London, 1960 —), and *Scholarly books in America* (Chicago, later New York, 1959 —).

American Library Association, The. **ALA index: an index to general literature, biographical, historical, and literary essays and sketches, reports and publications of boards and societies dealing with education** . . . by William I. Fletcher, 2nd ed., greatly enlarged. Boston and Chicago, 1901. Supplement, 1900-10. Chicago, 1914.

A subject index that tries to do for books of essays and general literature what Poole's *Index* does for periodicals. Indexes essays and similar collections of critical, biographical and other monographs. Continued by the *Essay and general literature index*.

Indexing of composite books was continued in the *Readers' guide* to 1914. See under 'Background: general reference: literature: newspapers and periodicals'.

British books in print. London, 1874 —.

Title 1874 — 1965: *The Reference catalogue of current literature.* This is the official trade list; gives authors and titles of books in print at the date of publication. See also *Cumulative book index* below and *Paperbacks in print: a reference catalogue* (London, 1960 —).

Cumulative book index. Minneapolis, 1898 —, later New York, 1900 —.

Since 1929 has tried to be a world list of books in English. Referred to as *CBI*. Published periodically with cumulations to form supplements to the Library of Congress Catalog. Together the Library of Congress Catalog and the *CBI* form a comprehensive record of American publications since 1898. An essential reference work. Since 1928 has included all books in English wherever published. Arranged in dictionary order — authors, subjects, editions, titles, series, in one alphabetical order.

English Association. **The Year's work in English studies** (1919 —). London, 1921 —.

Annual survey, arranged by literary periods. A valuable guide to scholarship, although not up-to-date.

English catalogue of books, The (1801 —). London, 1864 —.

The period 1801 — 36 is covered in a retrospective volume, ed. by Robert Alexander Peddie and Quintin Waddington, (London, 1914). From 1837 is a contemporary list, published annually and then cumulated into larger volumes at varying intervals. Basis of the list is the monthly one in *British books*, the title

English Catalogue of Books, The (Continued).

since 1959 of the former *Publishers' chronicle*. See above.
The *Catalogue* is the standard English trade list. The *British national bibliography (BNB)* however is better for books since 1950.

Fiction Catalog: a list of 4,097 works of fiction in the English language with annotations. 7th ed. eds. Estelle A. Fidell and Esther V. Flory, New York, 1961.

Part 1: author alphabet. Part 2: title and subject index. Part 3: list of publishers.
First published 1908; annual supplements, cumulated periodically. Essentially a listing of outstanding novels with critical annotations.

Publishers' trade list annual, The. 1873. New York, 1973.

A collection of publishers' catalogues, arranged alphabetically by name of publisher. Indexes issued after 1948 when *Books in print* began publication, followed in 1957 by the *Subject guide to books in print*.
Books in print is an author-title-series index to the *Publishers' trade list annual*.
Subject guide to books in print: an index to the *Annual*.
Lists under subject the books listed in *Books in print*.

Publishers' weekly. New York, 1872 –.

Weekly lists of newly published books.

Quarterly check-list of literary history, The. vol. I, 1 (1968 –); vol 17, 4 (1975). Published by the American Bibliographic Service, Darien, Conn.

A quarterly list of books related to literary history, analysis, criticism, biography and bibliography in the modern languages.

Whitaker's cumulative book list. London, 1924 –.

Quarterly and annual cumulations of lists published weekly and monthly in *The Bookseller* and monthly in *Current literature*.
Lists books published in Great Britain and Ireland; details as to author, title, classification and publisher.
The *British national bibliography* is more useful for books since 1950, because of its close classification and full bibliographical detail.

Literature: Newspapers and Periodicals

Listed here are the standard catalogues, indexes and guides to newspapers and periodicals. They should be used in conjunction with the lists under 'Background: Ireland: newspapers and periodicals: general' and under 'Anglo-Irish literature: literary periodicals'.

It is important to make good use of periodical literature. To do so, one should work with three types of reference aids:

(i) The bibliography or catalogue of periodicals.

This is not an index to their contents, but a list of the periodicals that gives information about them: their titles, history, nature, editors, publishers and prices.

(ii) The Union list of periodicals.

This is a catalogue of the periodicals to be found in the libraries of a particular country or a particular region. Union lists are of two main kinds: those which list periodicals currently received and those which give lists of sets, with exact indication of what portion of each set is in the libraries listed. They are usually arranged in alphabetical order according to title.

(iii) The indexes to periodicals

These give a guide to the contents of files of periodicals, doing for articles in periodicals what the library catalogue does for books.

Indexes are an important reference aid, whether to periodicals, books, reviews, anthologies, composite books, or the publications of learned societies.

All three types of reference aids are to be found below and under 'Background: Ireland: newspapers and periodicals: general'.

Abstracts of English studies. vol. 1—. Boulder, Colorado, 1958 —.

> Monthly. Abstracts of articles in American and non-American periodicals on English literature.
> Arranged by periodical, with subject index in each issue.
> Useful bibliographical source.

Book review digest. New York, 1905 —.

> An index to reviews of current books. Entries for each book by author, with publisher, descriptive note, list of reviews, excerpts.
> Cumulated title and subject list, alphabetically.
> Monthly, bound annual cumulation. Subject and title index cumulated every 5 years.

Book review index. Detroit, 1965 —.

> Monthly, then quarterly cumulations. Among the periodicals indexed are some in the fields of general fiction and nonfiction, humanities and bibliography.

British book review index. Reading, 1976 —.

> Indexes British and Irish newspapers and periodicals.
> Bi-monthly, with annual cumulation.

British humanities index. London, 1962 —.

> Quarterly, with annual cumulations. Title 1916-61, *Subject index to periodicals;* see below.
> Essential bibliographical source.

British union catalogue of periodicals: a record of the periodicals of the world, from the seventeenth century to the present day, in British libraries. eds. James D. Stewart with Muriel E. Hammond and Erwin Saenger, for the council of the British union catalogue of periodicals. 4 vols. New York, London, 1955-58.
Supplement to 1960; Quarterly lists, 1964 — , with annual cumulations.

> Supersedes for most purposes the *Union catalogue of the periodical publications in the university libraries of the British Isles.* (London, 1937).

Catholic periodical index: a cumulative author and subject index to a selected list of Catholic periodicals, 1930 —. New York, 1939 —.

> Quarterly with biennial cumulations. Indexes by author and subject, 50 to more than 200 periodicals, published mainly in the United States, Canada, England and Ireland.

'Current bibliography (of twentieth century literature 1954 —.)' Quarterly. **Twentieth century literature.** Immaculate Heart College, Los Angeles, 1955 —.

> *Studies in English literature* has annual surveys of scholarship: *Nineteenth century* (autumn issue).

Essay and general literature index, 1900-33. comp. by Minnie E. Sears and Marian Shaw. New York, 1934.
Supplementary volumes. New York, 1941 —.

> An index to about 40,000 essays and articles in 2,144 volumes of collections of essays and miscellaneous works.
> Substantially a current subject catalogue. Essential reference work. Gives lists of essays by a given author, analytical material on a given subject, biographical and critical matter, criticism of individual books, information about collections of essays.

Hoffman, Frederick J., Charles Allen and Caroline F. Ulrich. **The Little magazine: a history and a bibliography.** Princeton, N.J., 1946. (reprint, New York, 1967).

> In two sections: 1. history, pp. 1-230; 2. bibliography, pp. 233-398, followed by a detailed index to titles, change of titles, editors, contributors, etc. The history gives a general survey of little magazines from about 1910, with discussion of the more important ones, many of which included the first works of

Hoffman, Allen, Ulrich, **The Little Magazine** (continued).

writers who later achieved prominence, and thus have a definite place in the literary history of the period. The annotated bibliography gives, in chronological order, detailed information about a long, selected list of these magazines.

Index to book reviews in the humanities. Detroit, 1960 —.

Annual. Humanities is interpreted broadly. Indexes large numbers of periodicals; now includes book titles.

International Index: a guide to periodical literature in the social sciences and the humanities. New York, 1927 —.

Covers the more scholarly journals and many foreign periodicals.

'Modern Drama: a selective bibliography of works published in English in (1959 —).' Annually in **Modern Drama.** University of Toronto, 1960 —.

New York Times index, vol. 1 —. New York, 1913 —.

Semi-monthly, with annual cumulations.
Carefully made subject index giving exact reference to date, page, and column, and plentiful cross-references to names and related topics. Brief synopses of articles.
Prior series, covering 1851 — 1912, New York, 1966 —.

Nineteenth century readers' guide to periodical literature, 1890-1899, with supplementary indexing, 1900-22. eds. Helen Grant Cushing and Adah V. Morris. 2 vols. New York, 1944.

Periodicals indexed are mainly general and literary, but some are included from special fields. Book reviews are listed under author entry only. More than 13,000 poems are listed under poems by title. Full entry is under author's name.

Poole's index to periodical literature, 1802-81. 2 vols. revised ed. Boston, 1891.
Supplements, Jan. 1882 — 1 Jan. 1907. 5 vols. Boston, [c. 1887 — 1908].

An important index to American and English periodicals, since it covers the longest period (105 years) and indexes a large number of articles arranged under subjects.
Use with *Poole's index, date and volume key . . .* by Marion V. Bell and Jean C. Bacon.

Poole's index to periodical literature (continued).

Supplemented also by *Nineteenth century readers' guide to periodical literature, 1890 – 1899,* by Helen G. Cushing and Adah V. Morris. See above.

PMLA: publications of the modern language association of America. Baltimore, 1884/5 –.

Cumulative indexes to vols. 1 – 50, 51 – 60, 61 – 79.
Has current bibliography of work on all modern languages and literatures. Useful for scholarly journals; a standard source. Since 1970 there are separate fascicles, including one for English, Anglo-Irish and American literature.

Readers' guide to periodical literature (cumulated). 1900 –. vol. 1 –. New York, Wilson, 1905 –.

Beginning with vol. 19 (1953), the *Readers' guide:* (a) indexes US periodicals of broad, general and popular character, and (b) aims to provide a well-balanced selection of US popular, non-technical magazines representing all the important scientific and subject fields.
A modern index of the best type. Has full dictionary cataloging of all articles – their entry under author, subject, and title when necessary – and full information in the references, exact date and inclusive paging, illustrations, portraits, etc.

Subject index to periodicals, 1915 – 1961. Issued by the Library Association. London, 1919 – 62. Annual. (Quarterly, 1954 – 61, with annual cumulations).

An English index, begun in 1915 under the title *Athenaeum subject index;* title changed, 1919, to *Subject index.* Ceased publication in this form with the 1961 volume. Continued by indexes covering special subjects: *British humanities index, British education index* and *British technology index.*

The Times. London. Index to the Times. 1906 –. vol. 1 –. London, 1907–.

Title varies: 1906-13, *The Annual index;* 1914 – Jan./Feb. 1957, *The Official index.*

–––. Palmer's index to the Times newspaper, 1790 – June 1941. London, 1868 – 1943. (reprint, New York, 1965).

Much briefer than *The Offical index* noted above, but useful because of the importance of the newspaper and the long period covered by the index. A good factual source.

Ulrich's periodicals directory: a classified guide to a selected list of current periodicals, foreign and domestic. ed. Eileen C. Graves. 10th ed. New York, 1963.

A very useful classified list of almost 20,000 periodicals from many countries.

'Victorian bibliography [1932 −]'. Annually in **Modern Philology**. University of Chicago, 1933-57, and **Victorian Studies**. Bloomington, Indiana, 1958 −.

Issues for 1932-64 collected in William D. Templeman, *Bibliographies of studies in Victorian literature for . . . 1932-1944,* (Urbana, 1945); Austin Wright, *Bibliographies of studies in Victorian literature for . . . 1945-1954,* (Urbana, 1956); and Robert C. Slack, *Bibliographies of studies in Victorian literature for . . . 1955-1964,* (Urbana, 1967).

Wellesley index to Victorian periodicals, 1824-1900, The. ed. Walter E. Houghton *et al.* Toronto, 1966 −.

Covers *Blackwood's Edinburgh magazine* 1866-1900, *The Contemporary review* 1860-1900, *The Edinburgh review* 1802-1900, *The Home and foreign review* 1862-64, *Macmillan's magazine* 1859-1900, *The North British review* 1844-71, *The Quarterly review* 1824-1900.

Willing's press guide, 1874 −. vol. 1 −. London, 1874 −.

Annual. Principal contents, 1964: alphabetical list of newspapers and periodicals issued in the United Kingdom, with the year of establishment, when published, price, publisher's name and address; classified list; London suburban papers; London addresses of provincial publications; provincial publications arranged under their own countries; etc.

Background: Ireland

Background: Ireland

Introduction

Most students of Anglo-Irish literature find it difficult to plan a course of reading that will enable them to understand the contexts from which the literature emerges. Throughout the modern period Irish writers have turned to myth and legend, to folklore and rural custom, to the distinguishing linguistic features of rural speech and to the heritage of Irish language and literature. All have felt the pressures of history, all have been affected by social, political, religious and cultural pressures. Their range and variety of response is reflected in the divisions within this section:

general reference	folk culture and anthropology
history: general	the arts
history: early	language: Anglo-Irish
(including archaeology)	language: Irish
history: modern	Gaelic literature
biography	(including mythology)
topography	newspapers and periodicals

The more a student explores these different areas, the more he will see their interconnection. The divisions enable him to work systematically and efficiently, to find particular titles, to read about particular topics. But there are no barriers between them: history, archaeology, mythology, topography, language and literature are all part of the human experience, absorbed by the imaginative energy of the writers, available to the exploratory energy of the student.

General Reference

The titles in this section may be supplemented by comparable material, such as encyclopaedias, directories and yearbooks, listed in the various guides for students of English literature mentioned in the introduction.

Department of Foreign Affairs. **Facts about Ireland.** 3rd ed. Dublin, 1972.

A pocket-sized compendium.

Eager, Alan. **A Guide to Irish bibliographical material and some sources of information.** London, 1964.

Titles not confined to bibliographies. Where there are no bibliographies, general works or articles in periodicals, containing information on the subject, are included; critical studies of individual authors are therefore listed. Entries arranged by subjects; author and subject indexes.

Encyclopaedia of Ireland. Dublin, 1968.

A useful general reference, with a section on the literature. Comprehensive survey in thirty-five sections, systematically subdivided, from geology to palaeontology, wild life, archaeology, history; bibliographies for each section.

Irish Free State: official handbook. Dublin, 1932.

Still a good survey of many aspects of political, social and cultural life; bibliography for each section; index.

Nealon, Ted. Ireland: a parliamentary directory 1973-74. Dublin, 1974.

Biographies of members of the Dail, Senate and Northern Ireland Assembly.

Who's who, what's what and where in Ireland. London and Dublin, 1973.

Useful, factual reference work. Has descriptive gazetteer of places (pp. 493-537); glossary, index.

History: General

Irish historical studies have developed steadily in the past forty years. Listed here are the standard general histories, each of which has a good bibliography, and a number of works of a general kind.

The *New history of Ireland* draws from the best scholarship of recent decades and is the most authoritative and comprehensive work of its kind.

The works of Evans, Freeman, Mitchell and Orme reflect an area of scholarship too often ignored by the student of literature and one that becomes more and more relevant to a full response to Irish literature as the writers themselves explore the land and the landscape more intently.

Central Statistics Office. **Census of population of Ireland.** Dublin, 1966.

————. **Statistical abstracts of Ireland.** vol. 1—. Annual. Dublin, 1931 —.

Cullen, L.M. **An Economic history of Ireland since 1660.** London, 1972.

A basic study. Last chapter brings the account up to 1971. Bibliography and notes on primary sources.

Dáil Eireann. **Parliamentary debates.** vol. 1 —. Dublin, 1922 —.

Daily parts followed by bound volumes, each vol. indexed. A similar sequence for the Senate. Often valuable in showing official attitudes to literature and general cultural values. See also the *Constitution of Ireland* (1937).

Edwards, Ruth Dudley. **An Atlas of Irish history.** London, 1973.

Maps and graphs outlining the history of Ireland from the earliest times to the present in visual form. Select bibliography, pp. 246-52.

Evans, E.E. **The Personality of Ireland.** London, 1973.

Deals with the three h's: habitat, heritage and history.

Fairley, J. S. **An Irish beast book.** Belfast, 1975.

On natural history, detailed, well-researched. See also R. Lloyd Praeger, *The Natural history of Ireland* (1950).

Freeman, T. W. **Ireland: general and regional geography.** revised ed. London, 1972.

The standard work.

———. **Ireland: its physical, historical, social and economic geography.** London, 1950.

A good basic study.

Hayes, Richard J. **Manuscript sources for the history of Irish civilisation.** 11 vols. Boston, 1965.

A valuable reference work. Entries classified under persons, subjects, places and dates.

———. **Sources for the history of Irish civilisation: articles in Irish periodicals.** 9 vols. Boston, 1970.

Entries are arranged under four headings: persons; subjects; places; dates. Entries under any one heading are arranged in order of the earliest date of publication; the same entry will be found in each of these sections where appropriate.

Hayes, **Sources for the history of Irish civilisation** (cont.)

Persons, vols. 1-5: includes persons, institutions, societies, titles, etc. such as are normally found in an author catalogue. Political and religious organisations are in the subject section.

Subjects, vols. 6 - 8: subject headings are listed at beginning of vol. 6.

Places, vol. 9: confined to places in Ireland. Places outside Ireland are dealt with in subjects section. Table showing arrangement of places is given at beginning of volume.

Dates: articles dealing with events related to a specific date, topic or short period are arranged in chronological order at the end of vol. 9.
An indispensable work.

Lydon, James and Margaret MacCurtain, eds. **The Gill history of Ireland.** 11 vols. Dublin, 1969 – 1975.
A series of compact, informative studies, with bibliographies.

Mitchell, Frank. **The Irish landscape.** London, 1976.
Comprehensive and compact, with emphasis on the natural history of man; essential to a complete understanding of the whole course of life in Ireland.

Moody, T. W., ed. **Irish historiography, 1936-70.** Dublin, 1971.
A bibliography. See also the annual bibliographies in *Irish historical studies.*

——— and F. X. Martin, eds. **The Course of Irish history.** Cork, 1967.
An excellent collection of essays. Bibliography, pp. 349-67; with chronology of events.

———, F. X. Martin and F. J. Byrne, eds. **A New history of Ireland.** vol. 3: **Early modern Ireland.** London, 1976.
A definitive work, with comprehensive bibliographies; includes literary, linguistic, intellectual and cultural matters; vol. 9 (1977) has extensive bibliographies. In progress.

Ó'Faoláin, Seán. **The Irish.** Harmondsworth, 1947. (revised ed., 1969).
A valuable account of a national civilisation; useful for its analysis of the contexts from which the literature emerged.

Orme, A. R. Ireland. London, 1970.
Geography in the sense of man's total relationship with land-scape. Good general treatment from prehistoric times to the present; bibliography.

History: Early (including Archaeology)

Modern Irish literature has drawn so deeply and so consistently from early and medieval Irish culture that it is essential to study the history and culture of these periods. Ultimately such investigation leads to a study of the European origins of early Irish civilisation, a direction also present in contemporary writing. That connection is but briefly represented here, although it is latent in most recent scholarship.

Our study of virtually every modern Irish writer makes us turn to the kind of scholarship represented in the titles listed below, as we try to identify allusions, assess their value and understand the force of past experience on the imagination of modern writers.

Archaeology, a branch of scholarship that has undergone rapid development in recent years, is included here, since the connection between history and archaeology is so close.
The connection between this section and 'Background: Ireland: Gaelic literature (including mythology)' hardly needs to be stressed.

IRELAND
Monastic Sites +

Tory Island +

+ Carndonagh

Pahan +

Coleraine •

Letterkenny •

+ Derry

Glencolumbkille +

Donegal •

Lough Neagh

Belfast •

Inishmurray +

Lough Erne

Nendrum •

Devenish Island +

Armagh •

Inch +

The Mullet

Rathfran +

Sligo

Duvilaun •

Rosserk +

Dromahaire

Carlingford •

Burrishoole +

Strade +

Boyle +

Clare Island •

Castlebar •

Shannon

Kells +

Monasterboice

Croagh Patrick

Ballintober •

Roscommon •

Fore +

Mellifont +

Caher +

Cong +

Multyfarnham +

Drogheda

High Island +

Ross +

Tuam •

Lough Ree

Boyne

Durrow •

Tara •

Abbey Knockmoy +

Athlone

+ Rahan

Bective +

MacDara's Island +

Galway •

Clontuskert +

Clonmacnois +

Barrow

Dublin •

Clonfert +

Gallen +

Aran Islands

Corcomroe +

Kildare

Kilmacduagh +

Shannon +

Portumna

Glendalough +

Iniscealtra +

Birr •

Wicklow

Ennis •

Lough Derg

Roscrea +

Nore

Moone +

Kilfenora

Quinn +

Carlow +

Castledermot +

Canon Island +

Glenstal +

Kilcooly +

Slaney

Scattery Island +

Limerick

Kilkenny

Graiguenamanagh +

Adare +

Holycross +

Kells +

Ferns +

Magharees +

Kilmallock

Athassel +

Cashel +

Jerpoint +

Ardfert +

Tullylease +

Suir

Ahenny +

Dunbrody +

Tralee •

Blackwater

Mount Mellary

Clonmines +

Kilmalkedar +

Lismore

Waterford •

Wexford

Reask +

Killarney •

Ballyvourney +

Cork •

Ardmore +

Gougane Barra +

Timoleague +

Skelligs +

Bantry •

Borlase, William. **The Dolmens of Ireland.** 3 vols. London, 1897.
Their distribution, structural characteristics and affinities in other countries; together with the folklore attaching to them; supplemented by considerations on the anthropology, ethnology and traditions of the Irish people; with maps and many illustrations. The first comprehensive survey; full of helpful drawings. Vol. 3 contains an index and the material from folklore, legend and tradition.

Byrne, Francis John. **Irish kings and high-kings.** London, 1973.
Social and political history; a pioneering and valuable attempt to make sense out of a confused subject; draws upon the relevant literary sources. Bibliography, pp. 308-16.

Coffey, George. **The Bronze Age in Ireland.** Dublin, 1913.
Still the standard work on the archaeology of this period.

de Paor, Máire and Liam. **Early Christian Ireland.** London, 1958.
An account of life and culture, with emphasis on the material manifestations; considers the monasteries, the life of the people, the art work, the Vikings, the Anglo-Norman influences. Carefully selected bibliographies for each chapter; many illustrations. A good introduction.

De Valera, R. and S. Ó Nualláin. **Survey of the megalithic tombs of Ireland.** vols. 1-3. Dublin, 1960, 1964, 1972.
The standard work, authoritative, organised by county; illustrated. In progress.

Evans, Estyn. **Prehistoric and early Christian Ireland, a guide.** London, 1966.
A gazetteer of the more important archaeological sites, with general introduction and illustrations. Bibliography, pp. 223-30, general and by county; glossary, index of monuments.

Filip, Jan. **Celtic civilization and its heritage.** translated by Roberta Finlayson Samsour. Prague, 1962.
On European Celtic tradition, mainly the archaeology. Excellent background to the Irish material. Gives an overall view of the Celtic world from both a western European and central European point of view.

Gwynn, Aubrey and R. Neville Hadcock. **Medieval religious houses, Ireland.** With an appendix to early sites. London, 1970.

A definitive picture of the vast religious organisation of medieval Ireland. Catalogues all the religious establishments from the time of St Patrick to the early seventeenth century. Bibliographical and other sources, pp. 15-19.

Index of places, pp. 111-79. Includes ordnance survey map of monastic Ireland. See Hadcock under 'Background: Ireland: topography', below.

Harbison, Peter. **The Archaeology of Ireland.** London, 1976.

Summary account of the state of field archaeological research of the past twenty years; chronological sampling; illustrations.

———. **Guide to the national monuments in the Republic of Ireland.** Dublin, 1970.

Practical guide; gives information and history about each monument and access; illustrated, sectional maps; glossary, bibliography and index, pp. 261-84.

Henry, Françoise. **Irish art in the early Christian period (to 800 A.D.).** London, 1965.

Followed by two other volumes up to 1170. Also good on archaeology. See under 'The arts'.

Herity, Michael. **Irish passage graves. Neolithic tomb-builders in Ireland and Britain** 2500 B.C. Dublin, 1974.

Describes the tombs, art, burials and grave-goods; attempts to reconstruct the everyday life of the people: subsistence, habitations, technology, industries. The introduction provides a useful account of previous scholarship.

Bibliography, pp. 295-304; a comprehensive bibliography of sources, including manuscript sources, since Lhuyd (c. 1700).

Herity, Michael and George Eogan. **Ireland in Prehistory.** London, 1977.

The first modern study of the prehistory; examines the economy, technology, burial customs, arts and society. Bibliographical Index, pp. 255-282; illustrated; index.

Hughes, Kathleen. **Early Christian Ireland: an introduction to the sources.** London, 1972.
Useful summary; supplements Kenney (below) and deals with more than the ecclesiastical. Chapters on archaeology, secular and ecclesiastical laws, the annals, secular and ecclesiastical writings, art and architecture. Useful bibliography for each chapter; index. See also Daniel Binchy, 'Secular institutions' in Myles Dillon, *Early Irish society* (1954).

Kenney, J.F. The **Sources for the early history of Ireland.** vol. 1., New York, 1929. (vol. 2 unpublished). (reprint, 1966). (1968 edition revised and introduced by Ludwig Bieler).
An introduction and guide to the written sources dealing with the period up to 1170; includes references to Ireland in the ancient writers of Europe and Britain. Covers all significant documents illustrative of old Irish life and civilisation. Contains much bibliographical information on each entry; has excellent general bibliography, pp. 91-109; indexed

Mahr, Adolf. 'New aspects and problems in Irish prehistory: presidential address.' **Proceedings of the Prehistoric Society,** new series, vol. 3 (1937), London.
Particularly useful for its bibliography, pp. 261-436.

Macalister. R. A. S. **Archaeology of Ireland.** London, 1928. (2nd ed. revised, 1949).
An important work within the growth of Irish archaeological studies. First edition has an index of topography by county and an excellent coverage of the pre-1928 periodical literature.

O'Curry, Eugene. **Lectures on the manuscript materials of ancient Irish history.** Dublin, 1861, reissued 1878.
A most useful pioneering account of the annals, the histories, the sagas, the poems and much else; full of information; indexed.

————. **The Manners and customs of the ancient Irish.** 3 vols. London, 1873 (reprinted, New York, 1971).
A mine of information. Each volume has a detailed description of the contents of each of its chapters; vol. 2 has a glossary of Irish words, an index of names and of places, and a general index.

Ó Riordáin, S. P. **Antiquities of the Irish countryside.** London, 1964.
The annotated bibliography, pp. 95-103, is particularly useful.

Ó'Riordáin, S. P. (continued)

——. 'Prehistory in Ireland, 1937-46'. **Proceedings of the Prehistoric Society**, new series, vol, 12 (1946), pp. 142-71.
Important bibliography, pp. 166-71.

Otway, Ruthven, A.J. **A History of medieval Ireland.** London and New York, 1968.
The standard work. Does not deal with economics nor with Gaelic Ireland, but provides a useful synthesis in the other areas.

Pochin Mould, Daphne. **The Monasteries of Ireland.** London, 1976.
A useful history, with an account of the different orders, an alphabetical gazetteer, pp. 140-81 and bibliography, pp. 184-8; illustrations.

Raftery, Joseph. **Prehistoric Ireland.** London, 1951.
Non-specialist and descriptive; with index and illustrations.

Ryan, John. **Irish Monasticism: origins and early development.** Dublin, 1931. (New introduction and bibliography, reprint, Shannon, 1972).
Good bibliography by Marie Kelly, pp 415-81.

History: Modern

The student of Anglo-Irish literature needs to have a clear understanding of the developments that have taken place in Ireland during the past two hundred years. At times the connections between literature and politics, or literature and society are very close; at times public issues and national events impinge upon the literature in a dynamic way. The result is that in order to understand the literature fully one must read the history.

The books listed below provide adequate background reading about the main figures, events and conditions in the modern period; their bibliographies point to more specialised work.

Beckett, J.C. **The Making of modern Ireland 1603-1923.** London, 1966.
A comprehensive survey, with useful annotated bibliography, pp. 462-79.

Bowyer Bell, J. **The Secret army: history of the I.R.A.,** 1916-1974. Cambridge, Mass., 1974.
The standard work; detailed account with extensive bibliography.

Caulfield, Max. **The Easter rebellion.** London, 1964.
A detailed account of the events that affected Yeats, O'Casey and other Irish writers quite strongly.

Chubb, Basil. **The Government and politics of Ireland.** London and Stanford, Calif., 1970.
The standard work, with bibliography.

Connell, K. H. **Irish peasant society.** London, 1969.
Contains four historical essays; the fourth, 'Catholicism and marriage in the century following the famine' has some useful relevance to Irish fiction.

————. **The Population of Ireland, 1750-1845.** Oxford, 1950.
A major and revolutionary contribution to the subject of population and food in pre-famine Ireland.

Coogan, Tim Pat, **Ireland since the rising.** London, 1966.
A useful pioneering outline of developments on a broad scale.

Edwards, R. Dudley and T. D. Williams, eds. **The Great famine.** Dublin, 1956.
A sound, scholarly work, with an essay on the 'Famine in oral tradition' by Roger McHugh.

Heslinga, M. W. **The Irish border as a cultural divide.** New York, 1962. (2nd ed. 1971).
Sees the partition of Ireland in relation to historical developments.

Holt, E. **Protest in arms.** 2nd ed. London, 1960.
One of the most useful accounts of events from 1916 to 1923.

Kain, Richard. **Dublin in the age of W. B. Yeats and James Joyce.** London, 1962.
Has a useful literary emphasis.

Kee, Robert. **The Green flag.** London, 1972.
A history of Irish nationalism from 1170 to 1923 with special emphasis on the period from 1798 to the Civil War. Makes good use of contemporary newspapers.

Larkin, Emmet. **The Catholic Church and the creation of the modern Irish State 1878-1886.** Philadelphia, 1975.
Deals with the challenge of nationalism and the emergence of a clerical-nationalist alliance of Parnell, the Irish Parliamentary Party and the Hierarchy.

————. **James Larkin, Irish labour leader.** London, 1965.
A full-length study of the life and career of this most important labour leader; the standard work.

Lyons, F.S.L. **The Fall of Parnell, 1890-91.** London, 1960.
Essential for an understanding of the division of the party.

————. **Ireland since the famine.** London, 1971. (revised ed., 1973).
The standard work; up to date and with extensive bibliography.

MacArdle, Dorothy. **The Irish republic.** Dublin, 1951. (5th ed. New York, 1968).
Detailed, pro-republican account of the 1912-25 period; the standard work, with informative biographies.

McCaffrey, L. J. **The Irish question, 1800-1922.** Kentucky, 1968.
Readable synthesis, with emphasis on nationalism; bibliography.

McDonagh, Oliver, **Ireland.** Englewood Cliffs, New Jersey, 1968.
Short sophisticated analytical history since 1800, with emphasis on the recent period.

McManus, Francis, ed. **The Years of the great test, 1926-39.**
Outlines the period from independence to the outbreak of war; uneven, but useful.

Mansergh, Nicholas. **The Irish question, 1840-1922.** London, 1965. (revised ed. 1975).
A commentary on aspects of the relations between England and Ireland; the standard work, with bibliography.

Nowlan, Kevin B. and T. Desmond Williams, eds. **Ireland in the war years and after, 1939-51.** Dublin, 1969.
Informative about the conditions in Ireland during an isolationist period.

O'Brien, Conor Cruise, ed. **The Shaping of modern Ireland.** London, 1960. (reprint, 1970).
A good general survey; studies of significant figures and movements. ∗

——. **States of Ireland.** revised ed. London, 1974.
A mixture of history, autobiography and political analysis.

Ó'Faoláin, Seán, **King of the beggars.** [A life of Daniel O'Connell]. London, 1938.
Brilliant, psychological study with liberal, democratic emphasis for the Ireland of Ó'Faoláin's own time.

O'Hegarty, P. S. **A History of Ireland under the union, 1801 to 1922.** London, 1952.
Lively, informative, partisan.

O'Neill, Thomas P. and the Earl of Longford. **Eamon de Valera.** London, 1970
The authorised biography.

O'Sullivan, Donal. **The Irish Free State and its senate.** London, 1940.
A reliable account of political history from 1922 to 1939.

Pakenham, Frank. **Peace by ordeal.** London, 1935. (new ed., 1972).
The standard account of the Anglo-Irish treaty negotiations.

Rose, Richard. **Governing without consensus: an Irish perspective.** London, 1971.
One of the several studies of Northern Ireland; well-balanced. For more complete bibliography see Richard R. Deutsch, *Northern Ireland 1921-1974: a select bibliography.* (New York and London, 1975).

Whyte, J. H. **Church and state in modern Ireland, 1923-1970.** Dublin, 1971.
Valuable for literary students, specially for the 1940-55 period; with bibliography.

Williams, T. D., ed. **The Irish struggle (1916-26).** London and Toronto, 1966.
An informative collection of essays. See also F. X. Martin, '1916 − myth, fact and mystery', *Studia Hibernica*, no. 7, 1967, pp. 7-126 for an analysis of the 'literature' of the Rising.

Woodham-Smith, Cecil. **The Great hunger.** London, 1962.
A lively and scholarly account of the great famine.

Younger, Carlton. **Ireland's civil war.** London, 1968.
A useful survey based largely on interviews with survivors.

———. **A State of disunion.** London, 1972.
Studies of Arthur Griffith, Michael Collins, James Craig, Eamon de Valera; useful introduction; with bibliography.

Biography

Since there is no dictionary of national biography and no comprehensive and reliable alternative, research in this area can be difficult. The items listed below may be supplemented by those to be found under 'Background: general reference: biographies'.

Students should note that official records of births, marriages and deaths are obtainable at the Custom House, Dublin.

Book Association of Ireland. 'Biographical works published, 1934-44, about Irish men or persons connected with Ireland.' **Irish Library Bulletin** 5, 1944, pp. 92-6.

Burke's Irish family records. ed. Hugh Montgomery Massingberd. London, 1976.
> The criterion for inclusion in the first edition (1899) was ownership of a 1000 acres. Now it is distinction in one period for more than one generation, either through the church, politics, the arts and sciences, the professions or land ownership. In the absence of a dictionary of national biography, this work is helpful.

Cokayne, George Edward. **Complete peerage of England, Scotland, Ireland, Great Britain and the United Kingdom.** New ed. Vicary Gibbs. *et al.* 13 vols. London, 1913-59.

Crone, J. S. **A Concise dictionary of Irish biography.** 2nd ed., revised and enlarged. Dublin, 1937.
Brief notes on notable, deceased persons.

Falley, M.D. **Irish and Scotch-Irish ancestral research: a guide to the genealogical records, methods and sources in Ireland.** Evanston, Ill., 1962.
2 vols: vol I: repositories and records; vol. 2: bibliography and family index.
Deals comprehensively with every phase of record searching in Ireland and in the United States. Includes sources of Irish material not in Ireland. Excellent book. See also D. E. Gardner *et al, Genealogical atlas of Ireland,* (Salt Lake City 1964); compiled from Philips, *Handy atlas of the counties of Ireland* (1885), and Lewis, *Atlas of the counties of Ireland,* which lists the various records and their location; has extensive gazetteer.

Irish book lover. List of names of Irish biographies in the *D.N.B.* 3 vols. 2nd supplement, 1912: *Irish book lover,* vol. 3, 12 (July 1912), pp. 205-7, vol. 4, 5 (December 1912), pp. 80-2, vol. 4, 7 (February 1913), pp. 116-17.

Lodge, John. **Peerage of Ireland.** revised ed. by Mervyn Archdall. 7 vols. Dublin, 1789.

MacLysaght, E. **Irish families, their names, arms, origins.** 3rd ed. revised. Dublin, 1972.
Deals with names and origins: bibliography in two parts: 1. Irish family histories, 2. General (including periodicals with material on family history), county, diocesan and local histories. Bibliography, pp. 316-36; detailed index.

Share, Bernard. **Irish lives: biographies of famous Irish men and women.** Dublin, 1971.

Strictland, W.G. **Dictionary of Irish artists.** 2 vols. Dublin, 1913. (reprint, 1968).
Includes painters, sculptors and engravers; with biographical notices, lists of works, and an index of portraits. (vol. 2).

Thom's Irish who's who: a biographical book of reference of prominent men and women in Irish life at home and abroad. Dublin, 1923.

Webb, Alfred. **A Compendium of Irish biography, comprising sketches of distinquished Irishmen.** Dublin, 1878. (reprint, New York, 1970).

Topography

One of the distinctive features of all Irish literature is the emphasis on place. In former periods the literature was frequently directly involved with the significance of place. The names themselves often embody historical and human events. And while at one time even the use of specific settings served to emphasise the uniquely Irish nature of the work, since then writers have also tried to invest different regions of the countryside with personal, familial, historical, racial and cultural significance. This aspect of the literature has been somewhat neglected, partly because of the lack of suitable and up-to-date works of reference.

The works listed here may be supplemented by many of those to be found under 'Background: Ireland: history: early (including archaeology)', particularly by the various gazetteers, such as those by Evans, Harbison and Pochin Mould which provide information on specific places. Additional information may be found in works listed under 'Background: Ireland: folk culture and anthropology', particularly by MacNeill in which there are references to specific places.

The emphasis on topography leads naturally to the concern with landscape so that the work by Evans, Freeman, Mitchell and Orme listed under 'Background: Ireland: history: general' is also relevant.

Bartholomew, John. **Survey Gazetteer of the British Isles.** 9th ed. London, 1943.

Identifies places; provides maps with county divisions; has etymology of place names and the population of provinces, counties and boroughs.

Census of Ireland, 1851. Dublin, 1861 (i. e. 1862).

General alphabetical index to the townlands and towns, parishes, and baronies of Ireland, showing the number of the sheet of the ordnance survey maps in which they appear. See introduction 'Census of Ireland, Townland Index'.
Followed by *Census of Ireland, 1871, 1901* and *1911*.

Gwynn, Edward. **The Metrical dindshenchas, parts 1-5.** Dublin, 1935.

For dindschenchas, i.e. legends, etc., explaining place names. See especially 'general introduction', pp. 3-114; index of place names, pp. 180-210.

Hadcock, Richard Neville, **Monastic Ireland.** 2nd ed. Dublin, 1964.

Published with pamphlet containing an historical introduction by Aubrey Gwynn and an index of monastic houses shown on the map. Also issued bound with the pamphlet under the cover title: *Map of monastic Ireland.*

Hogan, Edmund Ignatius. **Onomasticon goedelicum locorum et tribum hiberniae et scotiae: an index to the Gaelic names of places and tribes.** Dublin and London, 1910.

Mainly pre-Norman, but useful for identifying place-names.

Joyce, P.W. **The Origin and history of Irish names and places.** 3 vols. vols. 1 and 2, Dublin and London, 1869; vol. 3, 1920. (reprint, 1976).

A rich source of information, some of it speculative. Vol. 2 has index of names; vol. 3 has alphabetical list of Irish names of places.

Lewis, Samuel. **A Topographical dictionary of Ireland, comprising the several counties, cities, boroughs, corporate, market and post towns, parishes, and villages, with statistical descriptions . . . .** 2 vols. and atlas. 2nd ed. London, 1842. (reprint, New York, 1970).

Ó Foghludha, Risteard. **Log-ainmneacha. i.e Dictionary of Irish placenames: English-Gaelic.** Dublin, 1935.

Alphabetical list of provinces, counties, dioceses, baronies, electoral divisions, post-offices, rivers, mountains, lochs, islands, etc., with Irish equivalents.

Ordnance Survey of Ireland. **Catalogue of the maps and other publications of the Ordnance Survey Department.** Dublin, 1927. (revised ed. 1949).

See John Harwood Andrews, *A Paper landscape: the Ordnance Survey in 19th century Ireland,* (Oxford 1975).

The maps are indispensable for topographical research.

Shell guide to Ireland. Lord Killanin and Michael V. Duignan. London, 1962. (revised ed. 1969).

Alphabetical gazetteer, with emphasis on antiquities and items of historic and artistic interest. Useful historical introduction, bibliographies, glossaries and maps.

Folk Culture and Anthropology

Irish literature, in its origins within Gaelic culture, has been affected by oral tradition and a once widespread folk culture. The country itself was until quite recently predominantly agricultural; the origins of the modern state are overwhelmingly rural. The presence therefore of folk culture in the literature is of special importance. Here too writers have attempted to offset their sense of cultural diminishment by appropriating aspects of their rich heritage of custom, belief and oral tradition.

The material listed below gives ample evidence of this practice. Paradoxically, however, the connections between literature and folklore have not been investigated as much as one might have expected. The archives of the Folklore Department of University College, Dublin are among the richest in the world, the countryside is full of material relevant to the literature, and the writers themselves frequently point to sources for their work within folk culture and anthropology.

Such study also involves the question of language for which the relevant material under 'Background: Ireland: language' - both Irish and Anglo-Irish - may be consulted.

Borlase, William. **The Dolmens of Ireland.** 3 vols. London, 1897.

See under history: early (inc. Archaeology)
Vol. 3 deals with the folklore of the dolmens.

Aarne, Antii A. and Stith Thompson. **The Types of the folk-tale: classification and bibliography.** Helsinki, 1961.

Provides an ordinal number and a title as a label on each type; the accepted register.

Arensberg, C.M. **The Irish countryman: an anthropological study.** London, 1937. New York, 1968.

One of the first cultural-anthropological studies; a good introduction to Irish life and Irish rural custom; a good analysis of the cultural system, work, family life, loyalties and the values that connect them.

——— and S.T. Kimball. **Family and community in Ireland.** Cambridge, Mass., 1940.

A classic anthropological study.

Brody, Hugh. **Inishkillane. Change and decline in the west of Ireland.** London, 1973.

A study of the effects of urban capitalism on the traditional life of a parish.

Bruford, Alan. **Gaelic folk-tales and medieval romances: a study of the early modern Irish romantic tales and their oral derivatives.** Dublin, 1969.

A study of the development of Irish romances from a literary form to folk-tales; discusses their conventions, the development of individual stories and how oral transmission has affected their style, form and content. Relevant to writers affected by the oral tradition. See also Axel Olrik 'Epic laws of folk narrative' in Alan Dundes, *The Study of folklore*, (New Jersey, 1965), pp. 129-41.

Danaher, Kevin. See Ó Danachair, C.

Delargy, J.H. **The Gaelic storyteller.** London, 1945.

Rhys memorial lecture. The standard account of Irish storytelling and its background: describes the tellers, their repertoire and their style of narration. See 'Publication of Professor Séamus Ó Duilearga' in *Hereditas* (Dublin, 1975), pp. 425-31.

Dorson, R.M. **The British folklorists: a history.** London, 1968. Chapter 11, 'The Celtic folklorists: Ireland', pp. 431-39. Bibliography, pp. 442-60.

A discussion of their work; useful introductory summary. For a different view see W.B. Yeat's judgement on Irish tale collectors from T. Crofton Croker to Douglas Hyde in *The Celtic Twilight* (Dublin, 1893).

Evans, E.E. **Irish folkways.** London, 1957. (reprint 1967).

More comprehensive than his *Irish heritage* (1942). The standard ethnographic study; full of information about crafts, tools and customs. Bibliography pp. 307-12.

————. **The Personality of Ireland: habitat, heritage and history.** Cambridge, 1973.

An anthropogeographic view; a study of environment as a factor in human history, in the interaction of geography, anthropology and recorded history. A usefully imaginative synthesis of disciplines relevant to the literature. Bibliography pp. 113-17.

Hyde, Douglas. **Beside the fire: a collection of Irish Gaelic folk tales.** London, 1890.

In the preface Hyde comments on the work of his predecessors, gives his views on the Irish stories and tells how he collected.

Logan, P. **Making the cure.** Dublin, 1972.

Deals with folk medicine. Somewhat marginal in its usefulness to literary studies.

MacNeill, Máire. **The Festival of Lughnasa: a study of the survival of the Celtic festival of the beginning of harvest.** Oxford, 1962.

The main source is popular tradition as recorded in the archives of the Folklore Department, University College, Dublin. The most distinctive manifestation of this harvest festival was an assembly at a traditional site. This study describes the festival as it has survived in various places; gives its past history in each case; seeks to discover the ancient myths concealed in the stories and the religious concepts which informed the customs.

Appendices with texts of the legends, accounts of assemblies, list of sites, lists of Lughnasa and Lammas fairs, list of festival names, indexes of days and seasons, beliefs, customs and legends, persons in legends, places, historical references; authorities and sources sited.

An invaluable reference work for literary studies.

LEINSTER

Adapted from *A Literary Map of Ireland*, compiled by Maurice Harmon and designed by Jarlath and Susan Hayes (Wolfhound Press, 1977).

DUBLIN CITY

Samuel Beckett
1906-

Brendan Behan
1923-1964

Dion Boucicault
1822-1890

Austin Clarke
1896-1974

Brian Coffey
1905-

Denis Devlin
1908-1959 (b. Scotland)

Monk Gibbon
1896-

Oliver St. John Gogarty
1878-1957

Valentin Iremonger
1918-

Denis Johnston
1901-

Paul Vincent Carroll
1900-1968 Dundalk

LOUTH

Lord Dunsany
1878-1957 Shane

Francis Ledwidge
1891-1917 Slane

Mary Lavin
1912— Bective

MEATH

Aidan Higgins
1927- Celbridge

Richard Power
1928-1970 N...

DUBLIN

Dublin City

Kevin Casey
1940— Kells

Brinsley McNamara
1890-1963 Delvin

WESTMEATH

River Boyne

L E I N S T E R

OFFALY

Pádraic Colum
1881-1972 Longford

Maria Edgeworth
1767-1849 Edgeworthstown

LONGFORD

Oliver Goldsmith
1728-1774 Pallasmore

John Broderick
1927— Athlone

River Shannon

Athlone

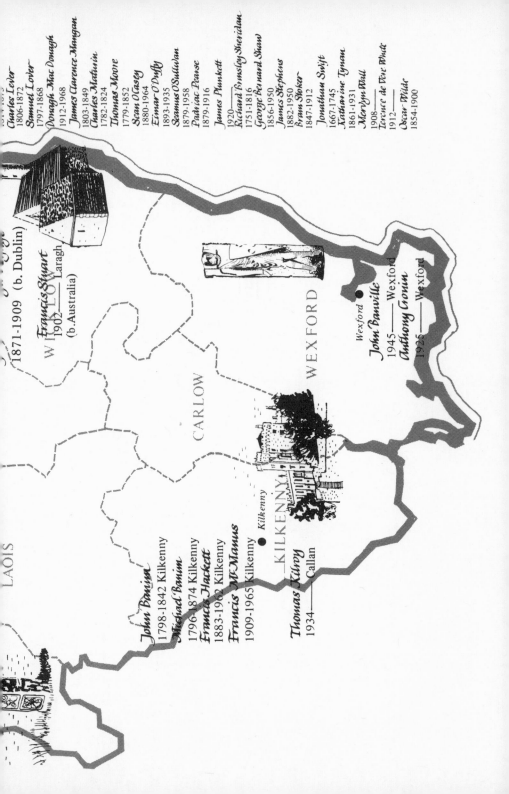

Charles Lever
1806-1872

Samuel Lover
1797-1868

Donagh Mac Donagh
1912-1968

James Clarence Mangan

Charles Maturin
1803-1849

Thomas Moore
1782-1824

Sean O'Casey
1879-1852

Eimar O'Duffy
1880-1964

Seamus O'Sullivan
1893-1935

Padraic Pearse
1879-1958

James Plunkett
1879-1916

Richard Brinsley Sheridan
1920

George Bernard Shaw
1751-1816

James Stephens
1856-1950

Bram Stoker
1882-1950

Jonathan Swift
1847-1912

Katharine Tynan
1667-1745

Mervyn Wall
1861-1931

Terence de Vere White
1908

Oscar Wilde
1912
1854-1900

1871-1909   (b. Dublin)

Francis Stuart
1902 ——— Laragh
(b. Australia)

WICKLOW

LAOIS

John Banim
1798-1842 Kilkenny

Michael Banim

Francis Hackett
1796-1874 Kilkenny

Francis McManus
1883-1962 Kilkenny
1909-1965 Kilkenny

Thomas Kilvy
1934 ——— Callan

Kilkenny

KILKENNY

CARLOW

WEXFORD

Wexford

John Banville
1945 ——— Wexford

Anthony Gorin
1925 ——— Wexford

Murphy, Gerard. **Glimpses of Gaelic Ireland.** Dublin, 1948.
An account of Irish folk poetry and of praise-poetry.

Ó Danachair, C. (Kevin Danaher) **In Ireland long ago.** Cork, 1962.
A useful introduction to material folklore.

———. **The Pleasant land of Ireland.** Cork, 1967.
A picture of the countryside at the turn of the century, its landscape, farms, dwellings, people and their everyday tasks.

———. **The Year in Ireland.** Dublin, 1972.
On calendar custom; drawn mainly from printed sources; with bibliography.
Deals with customs on significant days and times of the year, such as Samhain, May Day, Michaelmas, Midsummer, harvest, Lady Day, mummers.

———. **A Bibliography of Irish ethnology and folk tradition.** unpublished. vol. 1: authors; vol. 2: subjects.
The most comprehensive work; available in the library of the Folklore Department, University College, Dublin.

Ó Súilleabháin, S. **A Handbook of Irish folklore.** Dublin, 1942.
A guidebook for collectors and an encyclopaedia of Irish tradition, of fact and fancy, ritual and observance, custom and belief. Full of information for the ethnologist, the social historian and the literary student, on the matter of Ireland. An essential reference work.

———. **Irish folk custom and belief.** Dublin, 1967.
Useful in its range: house and home; farmer, fisher and craftsman; travel, trade and communication; the community, healing the sick, festival, pattern and pilgrimage; magic, the supernatural. Discusses the nature of folklore, folk custom and belief.
Good background material for the literature.

———. **Irish wake amusements.** Cork, 1967.
An account of the lively, merry wakes that were once widespread: storytelling, contests, rough games, imitative games, games of hide and seek, the keening, the opposition of the church to wake abuses, and consideration of the wider significance of wakes and their amusements. See also Reidar Th. Christiansen, *The Dead and the Living* (Oslo, 1946); bibliography of sources, pp. 175-81.

Ó Súilleabháin, S. (continued).

———. **Storytelling in Irish tradition.** Dublin, 1973.
Discusses the tale-types, the Ulster and Fionn cycles, the hero tales, the religious and the romantic tales (novellas), myths, legends (sagen), the conte fable and animal tales.

———, ed. and translator. **Folktales of Ireland.** London, 1966.
An important collection, with notes to each tale. Bibliography, pp. 293-7; index of motifs, pp. 299-304; index of tale-types, pp. 305-6.
Examples of international and national tales with a peculiarly Irish flavour.
Useful historical introduction by R.M. Dorson (pp. v-xxxii); evaluates the work of Irish folklorists and the role of folklore in literature, e.g. T. Crofton Croker, Samuel Lover, William Carleton, Gerald Griffin, Phil Dixon Hardy, Patrick Kennedy, Canon John O'Hanlon, Jeremiah Curtin, Sir William Wilde, Lady Wilde, Lady Gregory, W.B. Yeats, J. M. Synge, Alfred Nutt, Joseph Jacobs, Douglas Hyde, William Larminie, Seamus Delargy and Seán O'Sullivan.

———, and Reidar Th. Christiansen. **The Types of the Irish folktale.** Helsinki, 1963.
The Irish Aarne-Thompson. An index to the international tales in the archives of the Irish Folklore Commission, as of 1956. An essential reference work, with an excellent bibliography, pp. 10-26. For another detailed bibliography see Johannes Bolte and Georg Polivka. *Anmerkungen zu den Kinder – U. Hausmärchen der Bruder Grimm.* (Leipzig, 1932). vol. 5, pp. 52-64 on Ireland.

O'Sullivan, Donal. **Irish folk music and song.** Dublin, 1958. (revised ed. 1961).
Introduction to the nature of folk-music and its makers, the sources, the great collectors, the harpers, the songs and the dances.

O'Sullivan, Seán. see Ó Súilleabháin.

Thompson, Stith. **Motif-Index of folk literature: a class-ification of narrative elements in folktales, ballads, myths, fables, and medieval romances, exempla, fabliaux, jest books and local legends.** revised and enlarged. 6 vols. Bloomington, 1955-8.

Zimmermann, George-Denis. **Songs of the Irish Rebellion. Political street ballads and rebel songs, 1780-1900.** Dublin, 1960.

A discussion of songs of protest, street ballads, 'patriotic' songs, and of form; part two is a collection of songs from the eighteenth and nineteenth centuries. Bibliography, pp. 321-34; indexed.

Useful information for students of literature.

The Arts

Although the history of the arts in Ireland is uneven, the student of literature need not ignore it. His understanding of some periods may be deepened by an awareness of what was happening in music, painting or sculpture. Almost no study has been made of the interaction between literature and the arts, even though the connections between writers and other artists were close at times.

Tied in with such a study is the question of influence from one to the other, but there is the larger question of cultural preferences at particular periods. Those influences from native sources and from abroad that affect the literature also affect music, painting and sculpture so that it is possible to conduct complementary studies in the general area of literature and the arts.

Furthermore, when we consider the impact of the past on modern writers, their imaginative excitement is often caused not alone by the literature of a former period, but by its achievements in architecture, the illumination of manuscripts or the production of secular and religious ornaments.

Arnold, Bruce. **A Concise history of Irish art.** London, 1969. (reprint, 1971, 1976).
A general survey from the Celtic era to the present; with bibliography.

Bieler, Ludwig. **Ireland. Harbinger of the middle ages.** London, New York, 1963. (reprint, 1966). (German ed. 1961).
Excellent background for literary study; deals succintly with Christian Ireland, its monastic rules and cultural projection in churches, manuscript illumination, poetry and other arts.

Craig, Maurice. **Dublin 1660-1860: a social and architectural history.** Dublin, 1969.
The standard work; with bibliography and illustrations.

Flood, W.M.H. Grattan. **A History of Irish music.** 2nd ed. Dublin, 1906; (reprint 3rd ed. Dublin, 1970).
Somewhat patriotic, but attempts to cover the entire history of Irish music. Important as a starting point for further research. See also Donal O'Sullivan, *Carolan* (London, 1958), C. M. Fox, *Annals of the Irish harpers* (London, 1911), Ita Hogan, *Anglo-Irish music 1780-1830* (Cork, 1966), and Joan Rimmer, *The Irish Harp* (Dublin, 1969).

Henry, Françoise. **Irish art in the early Christian period to A.D. 800.** London, 1965.

———. **Irish art during the Viking invasions, 800-1020.** London, 1967.

———. **Irish art in the Romanesque period, 1020-1170.** London, 1970.
These three volumes comprise the standard, authoritative history, with illustrations and invaluable bibliographies. Footnotes frequently have informative descriptive comments; indexed. The work is relevant to literary studies; the footnotes and bibliographies often show which works were available to writers at particular periods.
See Hilary Richardson, 'Bibliography of Dr Françoise Henry', *Studies* 64, no. 256 (Winter 1975), pp. 313-25.

Hunt, John. Irish medieval figure sculpture, 1200-1600; a study of Irish tombs with notes on costume and armour. 2 vols. Dublin and London, 1974.

A pioneering study important to a wide variety of specialists, political historians, historians of culture, connoisseurs of armour and historic dress and historians of art. Vol 2 has 340 plates arranged by periods and types.

Irish Imagination, 1959-1971, The. Dublin, 1971.

An art exhibition catalogue with essays on recent directions in Irish painting by Brian Doherty and short essays on individual painters by contemporary critics and writers, including Terence de Vere White, Thomas Kinsella, John Montague and Pearse Hutchinson. Suggests correspondences in the period between literature and painting. In this connection see also Marilyn Stokstad and Mary Jean Nelson, 'The Arts in twentieth-century Ireland' in *Irish History and Irish Culture, Aspects of a People's Heritage*, ed. by Harold Orel (Kansas, 1976), pp. 271-89. Other essays in this collection are also relevant.

Leask, H.G. Irish churches and monastic buildings. vol. 1. Dundalk, 1955. vol. 2. Dundalk, 1958. vol. 3. Dundalk 1968.

Vol. 1: *The First phases and the Romanesque.*
Vol. 2: *Gothic architecture to A.D. 1400.*
Vol. 3: *Medieval Gothic, the last phases.*
The standard work.

Lucas, A.T. Treasures of Ireland. Dublin, 1973.

Commentary on Irish pagan and early Christian visual art up to the end of a purely native tradition about 1200; with bibliography and index.

McDermott, Matthew J. Ireland's architectural heritage: an outline history of Irish architecture. Dublin, 1975.

Highly informative, illustrated; wide-ranging and valuable bibliography, with index.

Petrie, George. Ecclesiastical architecture of Ireland, anterior to the Anglo-Norman invasion. Dublin, 1845. (reprint, Shannon, 1970).

Influential in its day.

Stalley, R.A. **Architecture and sculpture in Ireland 1150-
1350.** Dublin, 1971.

Deals with religious and secular works in the period from the
coming of the Cistercian monks and the growth of Anglo-Norman
influence; illustrations.

Language: Anglo-Irish

The Anglo-Irish language has been so little studied that it has been necessary here to list texts which are not readily available, and to rely on articles in periodicals. The subject is of particular importance for the light it throws on the literature. Successive Irish writers have tried to represent English as it is spoken in Ireland, traces of which are to be found even in those works which make no pretence to represent distinctive Anglo-Irish features of the language. In many cases the literature cannot properly be understood or evaluated without considering those linguistic elements which are derived from the contacts between the two languages.

Adams. G.B. 'An Introduction to the study of Ulster dialects'. **Proceedings of the Royal Irish Academy** 57 C (1948-50), pp. 1-26.

A discussion of Ulster speech in general, including the influence of Scots settlers. Dialects are determined on a phonetic basis.

Aldus, Judith Butler. 'Anglo-Irish dialects: a bibliography.' **Regional Language Studies.** . . Newfoundland, no. 2, 15 September 1969.
A pamphlet (176 entries) that tries to list most of the published writings on the English language in Ireland. Arranged under general and by province.

Bliss, A. J. 'The Development of the Anglo-Irish dialect.' New History of Ireland 3 (Oxford, 1976), pp. 546-60.
Discusses the eclipse of English in sixteenth-century Ireland, the emergence of Anglo-Irish and the influence of Irish on it.

———. 'The Language of Synge.' **J. M. Synge Centenary Papers 1971** (Dublin, 1972), pp. 35-62.
A valuable essay: surveys the history of Anglo-Irish speech, discusses its present-day peculiarities, and considers Hyde's attempt to use it as a literary medium. (See preface to *Beside the fire* and to *Love songs of Connacht*). The analysis of Synge's various attempts to write in Anglo-Irish dialect is a model of its kind.

———. 'Languages in contact: some problems of Hiberno-English.' **Proceedings of the Royal Irish Academy** 72 C (1972), pp. 63-82.
Somewhat technical in its emphasis on phonological and syntactic problems.

Burke, William. 'The Anglo-Irish dialect.' **Irish Ecclesiastical Record** 17 (1896), pp. 694-704, pp. 777-89.
A general survey; useful in its lists of characteristic pronunciations, old words, old meanings and 'peculiar' uses. The second part deals with grammatical points.

Clark, James M. **The Vocabulary of Anglo-Irish.** St Gallen, 1917.
Considers subject widely and well, but is very scarce.
Is particularly useful in analysing the differences in pronunciation, vocabularly, accent, accidence and syntax between Anglo-Irish and standard English. The discussion and illustration of Irish loan-words and of Old English and dialect survivals are valuable.

Curtis, Edmund. 'The Spoken languages of medieval Ireland.'
Studies (Dublin, 1919), pp. 272-92.
Deals with the beginnings of the use of English in Ireland. The
rivals for linguistic dominance were English, French and Irish.
Latin was the medium of law, literature and education. Interesting, non-technical essay; relates language to social and political
matters.

English dialect dictionary, The. ed. Joseph Wright. 6 vols.
Oxford, 1898-1905. (reprint, 1970).
Includes English dialect words still in use, or known to have been
in use during any time in the eighteenth and nineteenth centuries
in England, Ireland, Scotland and Wales.

Hayden, Mary and Marcus Hartog. 'The Irish dialect of
English.' **Fortnightly Review** 85, new series, (1909), pp.
775-85, 933-47.
Brief but valuable discussion of terms from Tudor and Stuart
English, from Irish idiom, with some observations on solecisms.

Henry, P.L. **An Anglo-Irish dialect of north Roscommon.**
Dublin, 1957.
A scholarly work on a particular dialect, with emphasis on
phonology, accidence and syntax. Bibliography, pp. 9-14.

———. 'A Linguistic survey of Ireland: preliminary report.'
Lochlann, 1 (1958), pp. 49-208.
Begins with some general observations on the rise of Anglo-Irish;
then becomes a highly technical analysis of linguistic matters.
Bibliography, pp. 201-4.

Hogan, J.J. **The English language in Ireland.** Dublin, 1927.
(reprint, Maryland, 1970).
The standard work; deals with English and Anglo-Irish in medieval
Ireland, with modern Anglo-Irish and its phonology up to about
1800. Provides examples, including some of the Kildare poems.

Joyce, P.W. **English as we speak it in Ireland.** London and
Dublin, 1910.
The first attempt at a detailed and systematic classification;
non-technical, full of examples of Anglo-Irish speech: idioms,
expressions borrowed from Irish, grammar, pronunciations,
proverbs. A useful reference work for 'strange' words and sayings
in Anglo-Irish literature. Chapter 13 (pp. 209-352) is a valuable
glossary of Anglo-Irish words.

Ó Cuív, Brian. **Irish dialects and Irish-speaking districts.**
Dublin, 1951.
Deals with the emergence of English and the decrease of Irish;
has maps showing the survival of Irish in 1851 and 1891.

Royal Irish Academy: Committee for the study of Anglo-
Irish language and literature. **Handlist of work in progress
and work completed on Anglo-Irish dialect studies.** Dublin,
November, 1972.
A bibliography mainly of unpublished work.

Taniguchi, Jiro. **A Grammatical analysis of artistic repre-
sentation of Irish English.** Tokyo, 1955. (revised and enlarged, 1972).
A good examination, based on Anglo-Irish literature. Analyses
and illustrates parts of speech, sentence structures, sounds and
spellings. Appendix (2nd edition): 'Studies on the structure of
the dialogue in Synge's plays' (pp. 269-387); discusses the rhythm
of Synge's language.
Bibliography, pp. 388-408; index.

Language: Irish

Some knowledge of the Irish language is essential for the student of Anglo-Irish literature. There is the obvious need to be able to read contemporary writing in Irish, little of which has been translated but much of which is relevant to developments in Anglo-Irish. There is the even greater need to be able to understand and to evaluate literary conventions, themes, allusions and linguistic devices which have been adapted from Irish literature. There is a fundamental need to read about the native heritage in its own language.

Behind the tradition of modern Irish lies the older heritage of medieval and old Irish. A knowledge of modern Irish is helpful, but in fact Old Irish is virtually a different language. Much of the literary material has been translated so that it is possible to acquire a good understanding of the old literature through the translations; here too it is advisable to acquire some knowledge of the original language.

Corkery, Daniel. **The Fortunes of the Irish language.** Cork, 1946. (reprint, 1968).
> A personal view of the history of the language and its role in Irish society from the earliest times to the present.

de Bhaldraithe, Tomás. **English-Irish dictionary.** Dublin, 1959.

De Fréine, Seán, **The Great silence.** Dublin, 1965.
About the economic and cultural factors affecting the language, specially since the great famine. Interesting history of the language. For other relevant articles see Bromwich, (nos. 121-29), and 'Background: Ireland: Gaelic literature including mythology' below.

Dinneen, Patrick Stephen. **Irish-English dictionary; being a thesaurus of the words, phrases and idioms of the modern Irish language.** New ed. revised and enlarged. Dublin, 1927. (reprint, 1965).
Outdated, but influential at the time of the Irish Literary Revival; an indispensable aid to the literary language. Retains old spelling.

Greene, David. **The Irish language.** Dublin, 1966. (reprint, 1972).
Deals mainly with the structure of the Irish language and its historical evolution.

Ó Cuív, Brian, ed. **A View of the Irish language.** Dublin, 1969.
Twelve essays on literary and linguistic matters, including one on 'Irish literary tradition' by Proinsias MacCana, 'Irish oral tradition' by Seán Ó Súilleabháin and 'Twentieth century Irish literature' by Gearóid S. MacEoin.

Royal Irish Academy. **Dictionary of the Irish language: based mainly on old and middle Irish materials.** gen. ed. Osborn Bergin. fascicles 1-4. Dublin, 1913-57.

———. **Contributions to a dictionary of the Irish language.** Dublin, (1939) – 1964. gen. ed., E. G. Quinn from 1953.
These are complementary publications constituting a comprehensive dictionary of early Irish.

Gaelic Literature (including Mythology)

Modern Irish literature is a literature in two languages, Irish and English, for while it is customary to study them separately, they belong to the same cultural heritage and ought to be studied together. Those who write in English frequently draw upon the Gaelic tradition with which they express their sense of identity through translations, the use of Gaelic prosody and other conventions, and through a similarity of theme and sensibility. These affinities also cause them to draw upon the sources of Old and Medieval Irish literature and mythology.

It is therefore essential to know Gaelic literature and to gain access to the great body of material in the earlier periods which has been the largest single source for writers in the modern period.

The material listed below ought to be considered in conjunction with that under 'Background: Ireland: history: early (including archaeology)'.

ULSTER

Adapted from *A Literary Map of Ireland*, compiled by Maurice Harmon and designed by Jarlath and Susan Hayes (Wolfhound Press, 1977).

Seamas Ó Grianna
1891-1969 Rannafast

Seosamh Mac Grianna
1900——— Rannafast

Peadar Ó Donnell
1893——— Dungloe

Robert Greacen
1920——— Derry

DONEGAL

Flann O'Brien
1912-1966 Strabane

ULST

Brian Friel
1929——— O

Benedict Kiely
1919——— Dromore

William Allingham
1824-1889 Ballyshannon

William Carleton
1794-1869 Prillisk

Shan F. Bullock
1865-1935 Killynick

FERM

BELFAST

Joseph Campbell
1879-1944
St. John Ervine
1883-1971
Samuel Ferguson
1810-1886
John Hewitt
1907———
Louis MacNeice
1907-1963
Derek Mahon
1941———
Brian Moore
1921———
Forrest Reid
1876-1947

Patrick Boyle
1905——— Ballymoney

DERRY

ANTRIM

Seamus Heaney
1939——— Mossbawn

E   R

NE

Montague
Garbhahey (b. New York)

AE (George Russell)
1867-1935 Lurgan
W.R. Rodgers
1909-1969 Loughgall

● *Armagh*

Belfast City

River Lagan

DOWN

ARMAGH

MONAGHAN
McLaverty
Co. Monaghan

Paul Vincent Carroll
1900-1968 Dundalk

Patrick Kavanagh
1905-1967 Mucker

Bergin, Osborn. **Irish bardic poetry**. Texts and translations, together with an introductory lecture. eds. David Greene and Fergus Kelly. Dublin, 1970. (reprint, 1974).

An historic essay (1912) on the training and function of the bardic poet, the classical introduction to the subject, with an anthology, introductory comments on the poems and translations.

For an annotated list of Irish poetry (editions of texts, texts with translations, translations) see Bromwich, (nos. 376-409).

Best, Richard Irvine. **Bibliography of Irish philology and manuscript literature publications 1913-14**. Dublin, 1942. (reprint, 1969).

————. **Bibliography of Irish philology and of printed Irish literature**. Dublin, 1913. (reprint, 1969).

Indispensable reference works for information about material in Gaelic literature of any period: publications of such bodies as the Ossianic Society, the Irish Texts Society, the Royal Irish Academy; material in journals, editions, translations, topographical material, collections and so on. Vol. 2 has index of first lines of poetry.

Bromwich, Rachel. **Medieval celtic literature: a select bibliography**. Toronto, 1974.

An excellent guide to the native literary tradition up to about 1450, to bibliographies, collections, editions, facsimiles, catalogues of manuscripts, grammars, dictionaries, language studies, literary history, criticism, mythology, the four main cycles, sagas, poetry. Annotated.

An indispensable reference work, carries on from Best, emphasising work published since 1940.

Carney, James. **Studies in Irish literature and history**. Dublin, 1955.

Perhaps too scholarly for the non-specialist. The chapter on Suibne Gelt is useful. For further discussion of this legend see Bromwich above, (nos. 222-7).

————, ed. **Early Irish poetry**. Cork, 1965.

Mainly about religious and didactic lyrics of the eighth to the twelfth century, with one essay on the metrical Dindshenchas.

————, ed. **Early Irish literature**. London, 1966.

(Reprint of two booklets by Gerard Murphy, *Saga and myth in ancient Ireland* and *The Ossianic lore and romantic tales of medieval Ireland*, and of Eleanor Knott, *Irish classical poetry*.

Carney, James (continued).

———, ed. **Medieval Irish lyrics**. Dublin, 1967.
Anthology, selected and translated.
Introduction has comments on Irish metrics; poems selected are
among the best examples. See also his *The Irish bardic poet, a
study in the relationship of poet and patron* (Dublin, 1967).

Chadwick, Nora K. **The Druids**. Cardiff, 1966.
A study of the druids of the early Celtic peoples of Gaul who are
the earliest teachers and philosophers in Europe known to us outside the classical world of Greece and Rome. Alphabetical list of
the principal classical references, pp. [xii] — xxii.

Clár Léirmheastoireachta na nuaGhaeilge 1940-1965. Irisleabhar Muighe Nuadhat. Maynooth, 1966.
A bibliography of critical articles on modern Irish writing. See
also Frank O'Brien, *Filíocht Ghaeilge na linne seo* (Dublin, 1968);
first three chapters deal with the literary background to contemporary Gaelic literature.

Corkery, Daniel. **The Hidden Ireland: a study of Gaelic
Munster in the eighteenth century**. Dublin, 1925. (reprint,
1956).
An influential work throughout the past fifty years; almost as im-
portant for the reactions it aroused as for its insights into Gaelic
Ireland.
See L. M. Cullen, 'The Hidden Ireland: re-assessment of a concept'
Studia Hibernica, no. 9 (1969), pp. 7-47; also R. A. Breathnach,
'The End of a tradition,' *Studia Hibernica*, no. 1 (1961), pp.
128-50; Rachel S. Bromwich, 'The Keen for Art O'Leary', *Eigse*
5 (1945-7), pp. 236-252; 'The Continuity of the Gaelic tradition
in Ireland', *Yorkshire Celtic Studies* 4, (1947-8); and Gerard
Murphy, 'The Gaelic Background' in Michael Tierney, *Daniel
O'Connell: Nine Centenary Essays* (Dublin, 1949), pp. 1-24, for
a discussion of the clash of cultures in the eighteenth century.

Cross, Tom Peete. **Motif-Index of early Irish literature**.
Bloomington, 1952.
A supplement to Stith-Thompson, *Motif Index of folk literature;*
follows his method of classification and enumeration. For students
of folklore and custom and of comparative literature.

——— and C.H. Slover. **Ancient Irish tales**. London, 1936.
(reprint, Dublin, 1969).
A useful anthology of material much used by the writers: e.g
Book of Invasions (selections), 'Destruction of Da Derga's Hostel'.

Cross and Slover, **Ancient Irish tales** (continued).

the Ulster and Ossianic cycles, 'Vision of MacConglinne', 'Voyage of Bran'.

For an annotated list of Irish tales and sagas (editions of texts, texts with translations, translations) see Bromwich above, (nos. 347-75).

de hAE, Risteard agus Brighid Ni Dhonnchadha, eds. **Clár Litrideacht na nua-Ghaedhilge 1850-1936.** 3 vols. Dublin, 1938-40.

Vol. 1: books, first three pages on literary history; vol. 2: poetry in journals; vol. 3: prose in journals.

A bibliography of books, periodicals, collections of essays, plays and poetry (with index of first lines).

d'Arbois de Jubainville, H. **The Irish mythological cycle and Celtic mythology.** Dublin, 1903,

Based on the *Book of Invasions* from which it quotes extensively. See Rees below for more up-to-date interpretation.

De Bhalraithe, Tomás. 'Liam O'Flaherty — Translator (?)', **Eire-Ireland** 3, 2 (summer, 1968), 149-53.

A comparative study of the story 'Touch' for which there is an Irish and English version. The aim is to see which version was written first. This is one of the few articles which explore literary connections between the two traditions. See also his introductory note to 'Darcy in Tír na nOg', *Nuascéalaíocht* (Dublin, 1952), for a discussion of Frank O'Connor's use of the traditional Irish story.

De Blacam, A. **Gaelic literature surveyed.** Dublin, 1929. (revised ed., 1973).

Recent edition has additional chapter on twentieth-century prose and poetry and a brief list of suggested reading. Still the best introduction to Gaelic literature from the beginnings to the present.

Dillon, Myles, **The Cycles of the kings.** London, 1946.

Tries to include details that may be important for students of history, anthropology or mythology. Gives stories in summary form. Index of persons, titles, manuscripts and sources.

———. **Celt and Hindu.** Osborn Bergin Memorial Lecture 3. Dublin, 1973.

Authoritative synthesis of evidence from language, literature, society and religion.

Dillon, Myles (continued).

———. **Early Irish literature.** Chicago, 1948. (reprint, 1969).
Not a history, but a discussion of forms and content.
Deals with the four major cycles, adventures, voyages, visions and
the poetry, both lyric and bardic; index and titles of first lines.
Good introduction.

———. ed. **Early Irish society.** Dublin, 1954. (reprint, 1959).
Deals with the history and literature down to the arrival of the
Norsemen. Of the six essays, three are of literary interest: Myles
Dillon, 'The Irish language' and David Greene, 'Early Irish litera-
ture' and 'Early Irish society'.

———. ed. **Irish sagas.** Dublin, 1959. (reprint, 1968).
Twelve essays, each on a different saga, including the Wooing
of Etain, the Sons of Osna, the Feast of Bricriu, The Cattle raid
of Cooley, the Destruction of Da Derga's Hostel, the Colloquy
of the Old Men, the Pursuit of Diarmaid and Grainne.

———, and Nora Chadwick. **The Celtic realms.** 2nd ed.
London, 1972.
Useful general account of Celtic religion, mythology and litera-
ture. See Chadwick, *The Celts* (1970, 1974), and Joseph Raftery,
The Celts (1967), for further information.
See Rolf Baumgarten, 'Myles Dillon (1900-1972): A Biblio-
graphy', *Celtica*, 11 (1976), David Greene and Brian Ó Cuív,
eds., pp. 1-14. Myles Dillon Memorial Volume.

Dix, E. and J. Cassidy. **List of books, pamphlets, etc., printed
wholly or partly in Irish from the earliest period to 1820.**
Dublin, 1905.

Flower, Robin. **The Irish tradition.** Oxford, 1947.
Lectures on bardic and medieval literature, with one on the love
poetry.

Greene, David. **Writing in Irish today.** Cork, 1972.
A brief, informative account.

———, and Frank O'Connor. **A Golden treasury of Irish
poetry, A.D. 630-1200.** London, 1967.
Anthology with introduction and with comments on individual
poems.

Hyde, Douglas. **A Literary history of Ireland from the earliest times to the present day.** Dublin, 1899. (revised ed., ed. Brian Ó Cuív, 1967).
Incomplete in some areas and out of date in many respects, but not yet superseded; with index.

Irish Texts Society. **Publications.** London, 1898 —.
About 50 vols. with translations, including many sources used by Anglo-Irish writers. See Bromwich above, (no. 17) for details.

Jackson, Kenneth. **A Celtic miscellany: translations from the Celtic literatures.** London, 1951. (reprint, 1971).
Not confined to Old Irish, drawing from writings down to the nineteenth century. Good, accurate translations of prose and poetry, with useful introductory notes to each category: hero tales and adventure, nature, love, epigram, 'Celtic magic', description, humour, satire.

———. **The Oldest Irish tradition: a window on the Iron Age.** Cambridge, 1964.
Brief, authoritative account of the heroic age. It compares the social customs and the material culture as described in the Ulster cycle with those in Celtic Gaul, as described by classical writers. See Chadwick, above.

———. **Studies in early Celtic nature poetry.** Cambridge, 1935.
Translations, followed by good discussion on the characteristics of this poetry and the question of its origins. Tries to discover from internal evidence the different kinds of nature poetry, its composers and its purpose. Introduction has authoritative view on the imaginative qualities of the poetry. The following chapters discuss hermit poetry, elegy and fenian poetry, gnomic poetry and seasonal poetry; bibliography and index.

Knott, Eleanor. **Irish classical poetry, commonly called bardic poetry.** Dublin, 1957. (reprint, 1960).
Good, brief summary about the poets and their work, including metrics, subject, literary style and various kinds of poetry.

———. **Irish syllabic poetry 1200-1600.** Dublin, 1957. (revised ed. 1974).
Has a discussion of the different kinds of syllabic poetry, a description of the metres, an anthology of the poetry in Irish, with notes and glossary. See also her edition: *The Bardic poems*

Knott, Eleanor. Irish syllabic poetry (continued).
of Tadhg Dall O Huiginn (1550-1591), vol. 1, text, vol. 2, translation. Especially useful for the account in the introduction of the bardic poet and his work.

MacCana, Proinsias. Celtic mythology. London, 1970.
Wide-ranging and informative discussion of the gods and goddesses, the heroic tradition of the Ulster cycle, the Fenian cycle, sacral kingship and the underworld; illustrated.

Meyer, Kuno. Ancient Irish poetry. London, 1911. (reprint, 1959).
Includes selections from myth and saga, religious poetry and nature poetry.

Murphy, Gerard. Early Irish lyrics. Oxford, 1956.
An excellent collection. See his *Early Irish Metrics* (Dublin, 1961) for index of technical terms and glossary.

———. The Ossianic lore and romantic tales of medieval Ireland. Dublin, 1955. (reprint, 1971).
About the traditions of Fionn MacCumhaill and the Fianna, including the Colloquy of the Old Men; an indispensable account of the origin and genesis of the cycle.

———. Saga and myth in ancient Ireland. Dublin, 1955. (reprint, 1971).
An authoritative introduction to storytelling, mythological tales (such as the Battle of Moytirra), the tales of the heroic cycle and the King tales.

O'Brien, Frank. Filíocht Ghaeilge na linne seo. Dublin, 1968.
A study of contemporary poetry in Irish. First three chapters deal with the literary background.

Ó Cuív, Brian, ed. Seven centuries of Irish learning 1000-1700. Dublin, 1961. (reprint, 1971).
A study of Gaelic learning from the Battle of Clontarf to the Battle of the Boyne. Nine essays of which Seán Ó Tuama, 'The New love poetry' is the most relevant for Anglo-Irish literature.

O'Grady, Standish H. and Robin Flower. Catalogue of Irish manuscripts in the British Museum. 3 vols. London, 1 and 2, 1926; 3, 1953.
Index in vol. 3, 1953.

O'Grady . . . **Catalogue of Irish manuscripts** (continued).
These contain a wealth of interesting discussion of scribe sources and literary parallels. For further information on manuscript catalogues see Bromwich above, (nos. 49-57).

O'Rahilly, T.F. **Early Irish history and mythology.** Dublin, 1946. (reprint, 1957).
About the pre-christian period; full of information; useful for discussion of mythology, the structure of old Irish society, and the Cuchulain and Ossianic cycles. Studies the interaction of historical and mythological tradition.

Ó Tuama, Seán, ed. **The Gaelic League idea.** Cork, 1969.
Useful in its discussion of cultural contexts. See also his essay 'Dónal Ó Corcora agus Filíocht na Gaeilge'. *Studia Hibernica* 5 (1965), pp. 29-41.

Pigott, Stuart. **The Druids.** London, 1968.
Comprehensive and authoritative; good bibliography.

Power, Patrick C. **A Literary history of Ireland.** Cork, 1969.
A survey of Gaelic literature from the tenth century to the twentieth; some sections on Anglo-Irish literature.

Rees, A. and B. Rees. **Celtic heritage: ancient tradition in Ireland and Wales.** London, 1961.
A stimulating and imaginative interpretation, based on scholarly sources, primary texts and folk tradition. Perhaps the most useful work for the non-specialist.

Robinson, F. N. 'Satirists and enchanters in early Irish literature.' **Studies in the history of religions,** ed. David Gordon Lyon and George Foot Moore. New York, 1912.
An informative discussion of this recurrent topic, with analysis of terms and categories.

Ross, Anne. **Everyday life of the pagan Celts.** London, 1970.
A brief but authoritative survey of archaeology and art, religion and institutions of the Celtic peoples.

———. **Pagan Celtic Britain: studies in iconography and tradition.** London, 1967.
An important study of Celtic paganism.

Ryan, Desmond. **The Sword of light: from the four masters to Douglas Hyde, 1636-1938.** London, 1939.
Useful general survey, somewhat nationalistic in approach.

Seymour, St J. Drelincourt. **Irish visions of the otherworld: contribution to the study of medieval visions.** London, 1930.
Studies the visions found in Irish ecclesiastical literature down to the end of the twelfth century. Principal authorities consulted and sources, pp. 9-12.

Sjoestedt, M. **Dieux et héros des Celtes.** Paris, 1940. Trans. **Gods and heroes of the Celts.** London, 1949.
On mythology. Establishes two categories: mother-goddesses and chieftain-gods. A useful summary account, uses *Book of Invasions* as a source. See MacCana, *Celtic mythology* for some different views.

Thurneysen, R. **Die irische Helden- und Königsage bis zum siebzehnten Jahrhundert 1.** Halle, 1921.
The standard work; detailed analysis of the tales in the cycle; bibliography.

Travis, James. **Early Celtic versecraft: origin, development, diffusion.** Ithaca, New York and Shannon, 1973.
Interesting in its examinations of varieties of rhythm, form and ornament, the connections with Indo-European archetypes, and in its establishment of the indigenous origins of the ornament. For scholarly articles on metrics and poetic techniques see Bromwich above, (nos. 138-47).

Williams, J. E. Caerwyn, ed. **Literature in Celtic countries. Taliessin Congress Lectures.** Cardiff, 1971.
Lecture 6: Mairtín Ó Cadhain, 'Irish prose in the twentieth century,' pp. 139-51.

Newspapers and Periodicals: General

Newspapers and periodicals are a source of information that are sometimes neglected by students of literature. Apart from their obvious usefulness as sources of general information, they are essential to biographers, literary historians and bibliographers.

See the introduction to 'Background: general reference: literature: newspapers and periodicals' for a description of catalogues of periodicals.

Bowen, B. P. 'Dublin humorous periodicals of the nineteenth century.' **Dublin Historical Record** 13 (1952-4), pp. 2-11.

Brown, Stephen J. **The Press of Ireland.** Dublin, 1937. (reprint, New York, [c. 1969]).
An historical sketch and bibliographical account of the Irish press — newspapers and periodicals — with extensive annotations on the more important publications.

Brown, Stephen J. (continued).

———. 'The Dublin newspaper press: a bird's eye view, 1659-1916.' Studies 25 (1936), pp. 109-22

———. 'The press in Ireland. Part 2: some Catholic periodicals.' Studies 25 (1936), pp. 428-42.

> See also Stephen J. Brown, *Ireland in Fiction,* reprint, with introduction by Desmond Clarke (Shannon, 1969), pp. 335-44, for bibliography of Irish periodicals, defunct and current.

Dix, E. R. McC. Irish bibliography: tables relating to Dublin newspapers of the 18th century, showing what volumes, etc. are extant and where access to them can be had in Dublin. Dublin, 1910.

Hayes, Richard J. Sources for the history of Irish civilisation: articles in Irish periodicals. 9 vols. Boston, 1970.

> See under 'Background: Ireland: history: general' for description of this indispensable work.

Inglis, Brian. The Freedom of the press in Ireland, 1784-1841. (Studies in Irish history, vol. 6). London, 1954.

> Traces the relationship of press and state; shows how the idea of the freedom of the press developed and the ways in which restrictions imposed on the newspapers delayed their growth into a fourth estate. Specialist bibliography, pp. 236-48.

Irish Association for Documentation and Information Services [IADIS]. Irish Publishing Record. Compiled by the School of Librarianship. Dublin, 1967 —.

> Annual. The Irish national bibliography. Covers material published in Ireland (32 counties). Material comprises books, pamphlets, the first number of new periodicals, yearbooks, musical scores and works on music as well as government publications of general interest. A complete list of government publications published within the year is available from the Stationery Offices in Dublin and Belfast.

———. Union list of current periodicals and serials in Irish libraries, 1974. Compiled in the National Library of Ireland. 2 vols. 5th ed. Dublin, 1974.

> The 1974 *Union list* lists about 15,000 titles and 32,000 holdings in 74 libraries in Ireland (32 counties). Earlier editions in 1929, 1934 and 1965 list titles and holdings in Dublin special libraries, while the 1972 edition lists titles and holdings in 49 libraries in the Republic of Ireland.

Madden, R. H. **History of Irish periodical literature from the end of the 17th to the middle of the 19th century, its origin, progress, and results, with notices of remarkable persons connected with the press in Ireland during the past two centuries.** 2 vols. Dublin, 1867. (reprint, New York, 1968).

Manuscript notes towards a 3rd vol. covering the period 1800-40, are in the Gilbert collection, Pearse Street Public Library, Dublin.

The approach in this work is mainly bibliographical and biographical and there is a nationalistic emphasis throughout. Valuable as a preliminary exploration, but poorly organised.

Munter, R.L. **A Handlist of Irish newspapers, 1685-1750.** (Cambridge Bibliographical Society monograph, no. 4). London, 1960.

Catalogues the vast majority of papers published during the period and certainly those of which copies are known to be extant. It is a finding list representing the main repositories in Britain and Ireland.

———. **The History of the Irish newspaper, 1685-1760.** Cambridge, 1967.

Really a history of the Dublin newspaper press, since newspapers were produced mainly in Dublin for the English-speaking Ascendancy class. Traces their growth and nature up to 1760 when provincial papers began to flourish outside Dublin.

Power, John. **List of Irish periodical publications (chiefly literary) from 1729 to the present time.** London, 1866.

250 copies printed; appeared originally in part in *Notes and Queries*, March — April 1866, and in *Ir. Lit. Inquirer*, no. 4, (1866), with additions and corrections.

Anglo-Irish Literature

Anglo-Irish Literature

Introduction

The emphasis in this section is not on primary works, but on literary history, reference material and bibliographies. It is divided into six parts:

Anglo-Irish literature:

general   drama

poetry   individual authors: bibliographies

fiction   literary periodicals

Since there is no authoritative history of the literature, the important alternatives are listed whether in histories of English literature or histories of certain periods, movements or genres within Anglo-Irish literature itself. The same holds true for the selection of bibliographies, serials and indexes. On the whole, works of criticism are excluded, except where there has been an effort to provide a wide chronological coverage.

General

American Committee for Irish Studies. **Newsletter.** vol. 1 —.
Milwaukee, 1970 —.
Annual bibliography in December issue.

Arnold, Matthew. **On the Study of Celtic literature.** London,
1867.
See John V. Kelleher, 'Matthew Arnold and the Celtic Revival' in
Perspectives of Criticism, ed. Harry Levin (Harvard, 1950), and
Rachel Bromwich, *Matthew Arnold and Celtic literature: a retro-
spect,* 1865-1965 (Oxford, 1965).

Baugh, Albert C. et al. **A Literary history of Ireland.** 2nd
ed. New York, 1967. Also published in 4 vols.
2nd ed. contains extensive bibliographical supplements. Good
on Irish writers; the best of the standard literary histories.

**Bibliotheca Celtica: a register of publications relating to
Wales and the Celtic peoples and languages.** Annual (1910-
28); new series, (1929-52); 3rd series, 1 —, 1953 —.
Has a section on Anglo-Irish literature.

Book Association of Ireland. Bibliography and miscellaneous
literature; plays and poetry. Ir. Lib. Bull. 7 (1946), pp.
36-7. Bibliography and miscellaneous literature (book list).
Ir. Lib. Bull. 6 (1945), pp. 142-3.

Books Ireland. A monthly review. Dublin, 1976 —.
Review of Irish-interest books published in Ireland and abroad; bibliographical lists.

Boyd, Ernest A. Ireland's literary renaissance. Dublin, 1916. (revised, 1922, 1968).
The standard history of the period. Deals comprehensively with poetry, fiction and drama; begins in early nineteenth century. Essential history. Bibliography, pp. 401-45.

British National Bibliography, The. London, 1950 —.
Weekly; cumulated quarterly and annually. Cumulative indexes and subject catalogue published every five years. Arranged by subjects. Includes Irish writers. Tries to list and describe every new work published in Great Britain and Ireland. Does not include periodicals, apart from first issue.
An indispensable reference work.

Brown, Malcolm. The Politics of Irish literature from Thomas Davis to W. B. Yeats. London, 1972.
A pioneering interdisciplinary account of the literature and its political and historical contexts. Based on primary, contemporary sources and on the best available scholarship. Bibliography, pp. 412-15.

Brown, Stephen James. A Guide to books on Ireland. Dublin, 1912.
Vol. 1, prose literature, poetry, music and plays.
Arranged by collections, prose, poetry, music, plays, including critical studies and biographies; indexed. Descriptive comments on each entry; useful for research.

Cambridge bibliography of English literature, The. ed. F. W. Bateson. 4 vols. Cambridge, 1940.
Anglo-Irish bibliography in vol. 3 (1800-1900), cols. 1045-67.
See the *New Cambridge Bibliography* for twentieth-century writers. An essential reference work.

Cambridge history of English Literature, The. ed. A. W. Ward and A. R. Waller. 15 vols. Cambridge and New York, 1907-18. (reprint, 1932-33, without the bibliographies).

Concise Cambridge bibliography of English Literature, The. 600-1950. ed. George Watson. Cambridge, 1958.
Includes major Anglo-Irish writers.

Contemporary authors: a bio-bibliographical guide to current authors and their works. ed. James M. Ethridge. Detroit, 1962 —.
Published semi-annually, with cumulated indexes.
Includes Irish writers.

Contemporary writers of the English language. ed. James Vinson. London, 1970-73.
3 vols.: contemporary poets, contemporary novelists and contemporary dramatists.
Contains biographies, good bibliographies and identification of manuscript locations. Revised every three years. Good on Irish writers.

Cutler, Bradley Dwayne and V. Stiles. Modern British authors, their first editions. London, 1930.
Includes Dunsany, Moore, Shaw, Stephens, Wilde, Yeats.

Daiches, David. The Present age after 1920. (Introduction to Irish literature, vol. 5). London, 1958.
Has brief bibliographies of many Irish writers.

Dunn, Douglas, ed. Two decades of Irish writing: a critical survey. Manchester, 1975.
Emphasis on modern poets, less on fiction; drama is not considered.

Études Irlandaises. Revue Francaise D'Histoire, civilisation et littérature de l'Irlande. no. 4, 1975 —. C.E.R.I.U.L., Lille.
'The year's work in Anglo-Irish studies' by Patrick Rafroidi, pp. 157-211; a bibliography; annual.

Fraser, G.S. The Modern writer and his world. revised ed. New York, 1975.
Places Irish writers in a survey of twentieth-century literature.

Harmon, Maurice. Modern Irish literature 1800-1967: a reader's guide. Dublin, 1967.
Has chronological listings of works according to genre and subject; publication dates are not always first editions.

Howard-Hill, T.H. **Index to British bibliography**. vol. 1: bibliographies of British literary bibliographies. Oxford, 1969.
Good section on Ireland, pp. 101-12.
Over thirty bibliographies of individual Irish writers.

Howarth, Herbert. **The Irish writers 1880-1940: literature under Parnell's star**. London, 1958.
Emphasis on George Moore, Lady Gregory, W. B. Yeats, AE., J. M. Synge, James Joyce.

Kersnowski, Frank, C. W. Spinks and Laird Loomis. **A Bibliography of modern Irish and Anglo-Irish literature**. San Antonio, 1976.
A checklist of sixty-one individual writers.

MacDonagh, Thomas. **Literature in Ireland: studies Irish and Anglo-Irish**. Dublin, 1916.
Attempts to examine the two traditions; influential, specially for its consideration of the 'Irish mode' in Anglo-Irish poetry.

Marcus, Phillip L. **Yeats and the beginning of the Irish renaissance**. Ithaca and London, 1970.
Considers Yeats within the Irish tradition in a wide sense and in relation to most of his early contemporaries: Katharine Tynan, Nora Hopper, John Todhunter, T. W. Rolleston, George Armstrong, Lionel Johnson, AE., Douglas Hyde, William Larminie.

Mellown, Elgin W. **A Descriptive catalogue of the bibliographies of twentieth century British writers**. Troy, New York, 1972.
Includes Irish writers born since 1840 and publishing after c.1890. Lists both primary and secondary material.

Mercier, Vivian. **The Irish comic tradition**. Oxford, 1962. (revised ed., 1969).
Considers the subject mainly under types of humour, e.g. fantasy, macabre, grotesque, wit, satire.

Millett, Fred B. **Contemporary British literature: a critical survey and 232 author-bibliographies**. 3rd revised and enlarged ed. based on the 2nd revised and enlarged edition. eds. John M. Manley and Edith Rickert. London, 1935.

Millett, **Contemporary British literature** (continued).
Each entry has short biography, bibliography, studies and re-
views. Includes: Elizabeth Bowen, Padraic Colum, Daniel
Corkery, Lord Dunsany, St John Ervine, Lady Gregory,
Katharine Tynan, Douglas Hyde, James Joyce, George Moore,
T. C. Murray, Seán O'Casey, Seán O'Faoláin, Liam O'Flaherty,
Lennox Robinson, George W. Russell (AE), George Bernard
Shaw, James Stephens, Francis Stuart, W. B. Yeats.

Modern Humanities Research Association. **Annual bibliography of English language and literature (1920 –)**. Cambridge, 1921.
Includes best known Irish writers.

Modern Language Association of America. **International
bibliography of books and articles on the modern languages
and literature.** New York, 1922 –.
Before 1956 was limited to American scholars.
Up to 1970 was published as part of PMLA. Now published
annually in separate fascicles, one of which has English, Anglo-
Irish and American literature as subject.

Moody, T. W., F. X. Martin and F. J. Byrne, eds. **A New
history of Ireland.** 9 vols. London, 1976 –. In progress.
Deals with literary, cultural and social matters; bibliography in
each vol.; general bibliography in vol. 9.

New Cambridge Bibliography of English Literature, The. In
progress.
Vol. 3, ed. George Watson, covering the nineteenth century, was
issued in 1969.
Section on Anglo-Irish literature: columns, 1885-1948.
Vol. 4, ed. I. R. Wilson, dealing with 1900-1950, includes Irish
writers.

New century handbook of English literature, The. ed. Clarence L. Barnhart. revised ed. New York, 1967.
Includes Irish writers.

O'Connor, Frank. **The Backward look: a survey of Irish
literature.** London, 1967.
Spans the whole course of Gaelic and Anglo-Irish literature.
The argument is flawed and the treatment is selective, but the
discussion is stimulating. See review by Proinsias MacCana, *Studia
Hibernica*, no. 8 (1968), pp. 151-63.

Oxford History of English Literature, The. Oxford, 1945 —.
In progress.

> Vol. 12, J. I. M. Stewart. Eight modern writers (1963) includes
> Joyce, Shaw and Yeats.

Pelican guide to English literature, The. ed. Boris Ford. 7
vols. London. 1954-61.

> Introductions to main writers and backgrounds; brief biographies
> and bibliographies.
> Vol. 7 deals with the modern period and 'Ireland's contribution'.

Rafroidi, Patrick. **L'Irlande et la romantisme: la littérature
irlandaise-anglaise de 1789 à 1850 et sa place dans le mouve-
ment occidental.** Paris, 1972.

> Has a particularly valuable bibliography, pp. 387-729.

Royal Irish Academy: Committee for the study of Anglo-
Irish language and literature. **Handlist of work in progress,**
no. 1. Dublin, June 1969 —.

> Annual. Useful list of books and articles, mainly according to
> author.

———. **Handlist of theses completed but not published.** no. 1.
Dublin, August 1973 —.

> Biennial. The most up-to-date list of its kind.

Seymour, St John Drelincourt. **Anglo-Irish literature, 1200-
1582.** Cambridge, 1929. (reprint, 1973).

> Deals with Anglo-Norman and English literature in Ireland.

Temple, Ruth Z. **Twentieth century British literature: a
reference guide and bibliography.** New York, 1968.

> Irish writers well represented: AE, Behan, Bowen, Colum, Eg-
> linton, Lady Gregory, Joyce, Moore, O'Casey, O'Connor,
> O'Faoláin, O'Flaherty, Robinson, Shaw, Stephens, Synge, Tynan,
> Yeats.

Poetry

Alspach, Russell K. **Irish poetry from the English invasion to 1798.** Philadelphia, 1948. (2nd ed. 1959, 1964).

A history of Anglo-Irish poetry from 1167 to 1798; also deals with the uses of Irish mythology and the material of Gaelic poetry by Anglo-Irish poets.

Brown, Terence. **Northern voices: poets from Ulster.** Dublin, 1975.

Establishes the contexts from which the literature emerges; a chronological study of individual poets: Samuel Ferguson, William Allingham, John Hewitt, Louis MacNeice, W.R. Rodgers, Robert Greacen, Roy McFadden, Padraic Fiacc, John Montague, Seamus Heaney, James Simmons, Derek Mahon, Michael Longley.

Clarke, Austin. **Poetry in modern Ireland.** Dublin, 1951.

Useful for the observations on Clarke's contemporaries, from Yeats and AE to Robert Farren and Patrick Kavanagh.

Farren, Robert. **The Course of Irish verse.** Dublin, 1948.

Concerned with the distinctively 'Irish' nature of the poetry.

Faverty, Frederic E. **The Victorian poets: a guide to research.** 2nd ed. Cambridge, Mass, 1968.

Includes William Allingham, Oscar Wilde, Lionel Johnson.

Granger, E. **Granger's index to poetry.** ed. William F. Smith. New York and London, 1973.

Indexes anthologies. Most Irish poets included. An essential bibliographical source. Constantly updated.

Loftus, Richard. **Nationalism in modern Anglo-Irish poetry.** Madison and Milwaukee, 1964.

General observations, followed by separate considerations of W.B. Yeats, AE, Padraic Pearse, Thomas MacDonagh, Joseph Mary Plunkett, Padraic Colum, James Stephens, F.R. Higgins, Austin Clarke. Bibliography, pp. 334-6.

Lucy, Seán, ed. **Irish poets in English.** Cork, 1973.

Examines the nature and achievement of Anglo-Irish poetry; includes essays by writers: Austin Clarke, Eiléan Ní Chuilleanáin, Bryan MacMahon, Benedict Kiely, Robert Farren, John Montague, Brendan Kennelly, Thomas Kinsella.

O'Donoghue, David James. **The Poets of Ireland: a biographical dictionary with bibliographical particulars.** London, 1892-3. (2nd ed. Dublin, 1912. reprint, New York, 1969).

O'Lochlainn, Colm. **Anglo-Irish song-writers since Moore.** Dublin, 1950.

A pamphlet with brief notes on the writers and their works; much of it drawn from O'Donoghue (above) and from Crone, *Concise dictionary of Irish biography.*

Rosenthal, M.L. **The New poets: American and British poetry since World War II.** New York, 1967.

Chapter 6, 'Contemporary Irish poetry' discusses Austin Clarke, Denis Devlin, Patrick Kavanagh, Thomas Kinsella, John Montague, Richard Murphy.

Fiction

Allen, Walter. **The English novel: a short critical history.** London, 1969.
A useful survey; includes Irish fiction.

Baker, Ernest A. **The History of the English novel.** 10 vols. London, 1924-39. (reprint, 1960).
Vol. 6: Edgeworth, Austen, Scott; vol. 7: The Age of Dickens and Thackeray (Chapter I: 'The Irish novelists', pp. 11-61); vol. 11, by Lionel Stevenson. (New York, 1967).

————. **History of fiction: a guide to the best historical romances, sagas, novels and tales.** London, no date.
Arranged under periods. Irish material: pp. 154-67, mainly nineteenth-century authors.

Bell, Inglis F., and Donald Baird. **The English novel, 1578-1956: a checklist of twentieth century criticisms.** Denver, 1958.
Useful reference work; has references for Bowen, Joyce, Moore, Swift, Wilde.

Brown, Stephen James. **Ireland in fiction: a guide to Irish novels, tales, romances, and folk-lore.** Dublin and London, 1916. (reprinted, 1969).
Arranged alphabetically under names of authors, with descriptive comments.

Chronological bibliography of English language fiction in the Library of Congress through 1950. ed. R. Glenn Wright. 8 vols. Boston, 1974.

Arranged by year of publication from the eighteenth century to 1950. Includes Irish writers; has a special listing of translators.

Flanagan, Thomas. **The Irish novelists, 1800-1850.** New York, 1959.

The standard work. First three chapters particularly useful on the background. Includes studies of Maria Edgeworth, Lady Morgan, John Banim, Gerald Griffin, William Carleton. Bibliography, pp. 343-51.

Foster, Jack Wilson. **Forces and themes in Ulster fiction.** Dublin, 1974.

Good critical studies of several novelists including William Carleton, Michael McLaverty, Brian Friel, Benedict Kiely, Forrest Reid, Brian Moore, Janet McNeill, Maurice Leitch.

Kiely, Benedict. **Modern Irish fiction: a critique.** Dublin, 1950.

A survey of fiction since 1920; with bibliography.

Leclaire, Lucien. **A General analytical bibliography of the regional novelists of the British Isles, 1800-1950.** Paris, 1950.

Useful coverage of Irish writers; index to Irish counties, pp. 384-7.

MacDonagh, Oliver. **The Nineteenth-century novel and Irish social history: some aspects.** Dublin, 1970.

A lecture on the theme of the Big House in fiction in relation to nineteenth-century history. See also Maurice Harmon, 'Aspects of the peasantry in Anglo-Irish literature from 1800 to 1916' in *Studia Hibernica*, no. 15 (1975), pp. 105-27.

Palmer, Helen H. and Anne Jane Dyson, eds. **English novel explications, criticisms to 1972.** Hamden, Conn., 1973.

Includes Bowen, Beckett, Edgeworth, Joyce, Moore, Murdoch, Shaw, Stephens, Wilde. Is a continuation of Bell (above).

Rafroidi, Patrick and Maurice Harmon, eds. **The Irish novel in our time.** Lille, 1976.

General assessments and surveys, with critical examinations of individual writers, such as John Banville, John Broderick, Richard

Rafroidi and Harmon, **The Irish novel in our time** (continued).

Power, Edna O'Brien, Christy Brown, James Plunkett, Francis Stuart, Benedict Kiely. With bibliographies of most twentieth-century novelists.

Sadleir, Michael. **XIX century fiction: a bibliographical record based on his own collection.** 2 vols. Cambridge, 1951.

Irish writers well represented: Edgeworth, Carleton, the Banims, Lever, Moore, Somerville and Ross.

Watt, Ian. **The British novel: Scott through Hardy.** (Goldentree Bibliography Series). Northbrook, Illinois, 1973.

Includes the Banims, Carleton, Griffin and others.

Wiley, Paul L. **The British novel: Conrad to the present.** (Goldentree Bibliography Series). Northbrook, Illinois, 1973.

Includes many Irish novelists.

Drama

Bartley, J. D. Teague, Shenkin and Sawney; being an historical study of the earliest Irish, Welsh and Scottish characters in English plays. Cork, 1954.

Has three chapters on the stock Irish character from 1587-1800; appendix with list of printed plays; bibliography.

Bell, Sam Hanna. The Theatre in Ulster: a survey of the dramatic movement in Ulster from 1902 to the present day. Dublin, 1972.

The best available account; with appendix listing performances at the Ulster Literary Theatre, the Ulster Group Theatre (1916-60); the Lyric Players Theatre (1951-71).

Clark, William Smyth. The Early Irish Stage: the beginnings to 1720. Oxford, 1955.

A history of theatrical activity in relation to the contemporary social scene; deals also with staging methods in Dublin and with the acting troupe at the Dublin Theatre Royal.

———. The Irish stage in the country towns 1700-1800. Oxford, 1965.

A continuation of the above; more emphasis on town life throughout the country; locates the theatres. Lists of plays, performances, dramatists, actors, actresses. Bibliography, pp. 383-8.

These are the standard works. See also T. J. Walsh, *Opera in Dublin 1705-1797: the social scene.* (Dublin, 1973); bibliographical list of first performances, index.

Duggan, D.C. **The Stage Irishman: a history of the Irish play and stage characters from earliest times.** Dublin, 1937.
> Has useful comments on plays on Irish subjects and on the evolution of the stage Irishman. See also Lewis P. Curtis, *Apes and angels: the Irishman in Victorian caricature.* (Newton Abbot, Devon and New York, 1971).

Ellis-Fermor, Una. **The Irish dramatic movement.** London, 1939. (2nd ed, 1954). (reprint, 1964, 1967).
> The standard study of the Abbey Theatre. Does not try to replace Malone. Gives chronological table of the main events up to 1904.

Fay, Gerald. **The Abbey theatre: cradle of genius.** London and Dublin, 1958.
> Reflections on the development of the theatre up to the departure of Seán O'Casey. Good on the contribution of the Fay brothers.
> List of productions, 1899-1958.

Gregory, Lady. **Our Irish theatre.** London, 1913. (3rd ed. revised and enlarged, Gerrard's Cross, 1972).
> A unique personal account of the establishment of the Abbey theatre and of its early aims and experiences.

Hobson, Bulmer, ed. **The Gate theatre, Dublin.** Dublin, 1934.
> A literary and pictorial history. List of productions, 1928-1934. Notes on members of the company.

Hogan, Robert, **After the renaissance: a critical history of the Irish drama since 'The Plough and the Stars'.** Minneapolis, 1964.
> An informal critical history; fairly comprehensive. Discusses Paul Vincent Carroll, M. J. Molloy, Joseph Tomelty, Denis Johnston, George Fitzmaurice and both the Abbey and the Gate theatres. Bibliography, pp. 259-74 of general histories and of individual dramatists.

Kavanagh, Peter. **The Irish theatre: being a history of the drama in Ireland from the earliest period up to the present day.** Tralee, 1946.
> Has some interesting details about seventeenth-century Jesuit dramatists, but focuses on the eighteenth and nineteenth centuries. For greater clarity and scope, see Stockwell, *Dublin Theatre and theatre customs 1637-1820* (1938).

Kavanagh, Peter (continued).

————. **The Story of the Abbey theatre from its origins in 1899 to the present.** New York, 1950.
Essentially from the foundation to the death of Yeats; with list of first productions up to 1949.

MacLiammoir, Michael. **Theatre in Ireland.** Dublin, 1950. (reprint, 1964).
Useful introduction, with illuminating observations on both the Gate and the Abbey theatres. See also 'We start a theatre' in *Irish Art Handbook*, (1943), pp. 85-92 for MacLiammoir's reflections on the Gate theatre.

McNamara, Brinsley. **Abbey plays 1899-1948, including the productions of the Irish Literary Theatre.** Dublin, 1949.
Dates and places of performances, with casts. Brings Malone up to 1948.

Malone, A.E. **The Irish Drama 1896-1928.** London, 1929. (reprint, 1965).
The standard history; drama in the contexts of political and nationalist movements. Appendix: complete list of performances, first productions, authors, plays.

Mikhail, E.H. **A Bibliography of modern Irish drama 1899-1970.** London, 1972.
The first comprehensive bibliography; tries to bring existing bibliographies up to date and to consolidate them.

————. **Dissertations on the Anglo-Irish drama: a bibliography of studies, 1870-1970.** London and Basingstoke, 1973.
Arranged by author.

Nicoll, Allardyce. **English Drama 1900-1930: the beginnings of the modern period.** Cambridge, 1973.
Good on Irish theatre. Part 1: a compendium; includes various Irish theatres; has bibliography. Part 2: handlist of plays by Hyde, Yeats, Lady Gregory, Moore, Martyn, Colum, Robinson, Murray, O'Casey.

Ó hAodha, Micheál. **Theatre in Ireland.** Oxford, 1974.
An introductory survey up to the present. Bibliography, pp. 157-60.

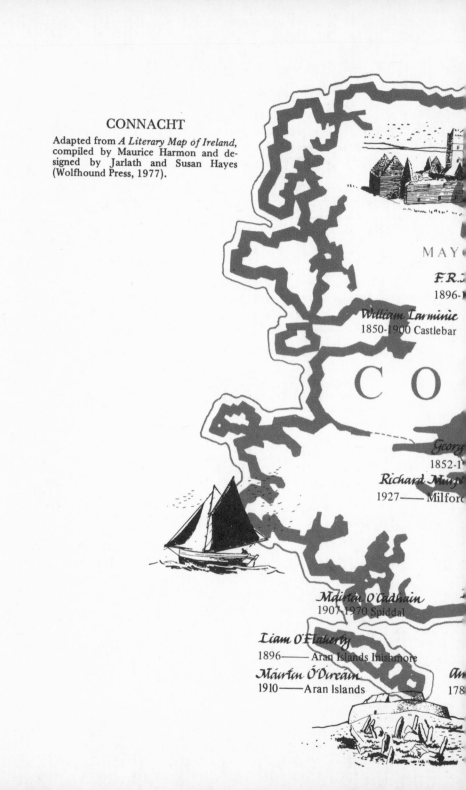

CONNACHT

Adapted from *A Literary Map of Ireland*, compiled by Maurice Harmon and designed by Jarlath and Susan Hayes (Wolfhound Press, 1977).

MAY

F.R.
1896-

William Larminie
1850-1900 Castlebar

CO

Georg
1852-1

Richard Murp
1927——Milforc

Máirtín Ó Cadhain
1907-1970 Spiddal

Liam O'Flaherty
1896—— Aran Islands Inishmore

Máirtín Ó Direáin
1910——Aran Islands

An
178

William Butler Yeats
1865-1939 (b.Dublin)

● *Sligo*

SLIGO

LEITRIM

John M°Gahern
1934- Knockvicar

Douglas Hyde ROSCOMMON
1860-1949 French Park

N A C H T

M. J. Molloy
1917——— Milltown

Hall

Thomas Murphy
936——— Tuam

River Shannon

Lady Gregory
1852-1932 Roxborough

GALWAY

Padraic Fallon
1905-1975 Athenry

Seamus O'Kelly
1881-1918 Loughrea

Edward Martyn
1859-1923 Tulyra

Galway

Galway City

O'Neill, James J. **A bibliographical account of Irish theatrical literature. Dublin, 1920.**
Pre-1800, pp. 57-88.

Robinson, Lennox. **Ireland's Abbey theatre: a history 1899-1951. London, 1951.**
Includes dates of production and complete casts. The official history up to 1950. Useful mainly for its factual records.

Individual Authors: Bibliographies

Introduction

There are two main kinds of bibliographies: a basic bibliography that is comprehensive up to a certain date, and a current bibliography that records the publications of a given period, frequently in annual cumulations and sometimes in specialist periodicals.

For most reference and research purposes the comprehensive bibliography which records books, articles in periodicals and other analytical material is the most useful.

For serious research purposes it is essential to consult the current or serial bibliographies, those monthly, quarterly, semi-annual or annual publications that record work as it is published. They may include poems, plays, short stories, novels, excerpts from novels, interviews, reviews, essays, as well as articles in periodicals.

In preparing a bibliography of a particular writer, the student should consult general sources — library catalogues, bibliographies of bibliography, dissertations, comprehensive and current bibliographies — individual monographs, specialist bibliographies and so on. By following the plan of this guide he can consult the essential reference material in a systematic manner.

Irish studies need to be strengthened in the area of bibliography: there are few comprehensive or current bibliographies and the supporting reference material is inadequate. Apart from the major figures, bibliographies of individual writers scarcely exist.

The following list of individual bibliographies found in periodicals and in book-form is offered with reservations as to the quality of many items. It should be noted that it does not include bibliographies in literary histories, critical studies, collections of essays or editions of the authors' works.

WILLIAM ALLINGHAM

O'Hegarty, P.S. **A Bibliography of William Allingham.** Dublin, 1945.
Privately printed; from *Dublin Magazine,* new series, 20, no. 1 (1945), pp. 42-52 and no. 3 (1945), 62.

Warner, Alan. 'William Allingham: a bibliographical survey,' **Irish Booklore** 2, no. 2 (1975).

SAMUEL BECKETT

Federman, Samuel and John Fletcher. **Samuel Beckett. His works and his critics: an essay in bibliography.** Berkeley and London, 1970.
See also James Mays, 'Samuel Beckett bibliography: comments and corrections,' *Irish University Review* 2, no. 2 (autumn, 1972), pp. 189-207.

GEORGE A. BIRMINGHAM

Mackey, W.E. 'The Novels of George A. Birmingham: a list of first editions.' **T.C.D. Annual Bulletin** (1955), pp. 14-16.

ELIZABETH BOWEN

Sellery, J'nan. 'Elizabeth Bowen: a check list.' **Bulletin of the New York Public Library** 74 (1970), pp. 219-74.

EDWARD JOHN BRENNAN

'Bibliography,' **Irish Book Lover** 8 (1916-17), p. 142.

JOSEPH CAMPBELL

O'Hegarty, P.S. 'Bibliographical notes (Bibliography of Joseph Campbell).' **Dublin Magazine,** new series, 15, no. 4 (1940), pp. 58-61.

AUSTIN CLARKE

Lyne, Gerard. 'Austin Clarke: a bibliography.' **Irish University Review** 4, no. 1 (spring 1974), pp. 137-55.

PADRAIC COLUM

Denson, Alan. 'Padraic Colum: an appreciation, with a checklist of his publications.' **Dublin Magazine** 6, (spring 1967), pp. 50-65; 6 (summer 1967), pp. 83-85.

LORD DUNSANY

Black, H.M. 'A Check-list of first editions of works of Lord Dunsany.' **T.C.D. Annual Bulletin** (1957), pp. 4-8.

MARIA EDGEWORTH

Slade, Bertha Coolidge. **Maria Edgeworth, 1767-1849: a bibliographical tribute.** London, 1937.

GEORGE FITZMAURICE

Henderson, Joanne C. 'Check-list of 4 Kerry writers — Fitzmaurice, Walsh, MacMahon, Keane.' **Journal of Irish Literature.** (May, 1967), pp. 101-19.

Miller, Liam. 'George Fitzmaurice, a bibliographical note.' **Irish Writing** 15 (1951), pp. 47-8.

F. R. HIGGINS

MacManus, M.J. 'A Bibliography of F. R. Higgins.' **Dublin Magazine**, new series, 12, no. 1 (1937), pp. 61-7.

DOUGLAS HYDE

de Bhaldraithe, Tomás. 'Aguisin le clár saothair An Chraoibhin.' **Galvia** 4 (1957), pp. 18-24.

JOHN KELLS INGRAM

Lyster, T. W. 'Bibliography of the writing of John Kells Ingram, 1823-1907, with a brief chronology.' **An Leabharlann** 3 (1909), pp. 3-46.

JAMES JOYCE

Beebe, Maurice, Phillip F. Herring and Walton Litz. 'Criticism of James Joyce: a selected checklist.' **Modern Fiction Studies** 15 (spring 1969), pp. 105-82.

James Joyce (continued).

Cohn, Alan M. and Richard M. Kain. 'Supplemental James Joyce Checklist, 1962.' James Joyce Quarterly 1 (winter, 1964), pp. 15-22.
Continued in subsequent years (fall, 1964, 1965; winter, 1966; spring, 1966; winter, 1967; spring, 1969).

Deming, Robert H. A Bibliography of James Joyce Studies. Kansas, 1964.

Parker, Alan Dean. James Joyce: a bibliography of his writings, critical material and miscellanea. Boston, Mass., 1948.

———. 'Addenda to James Joyce bibliography, 1950-3.' James Joyce Review 1, no. 2 (1957), pp. 9-25.

———. Addenda to James Joyce bibliography, 1954-7. James Joyce Review 1, no. 3 (1957), pp. 3-24.
Further addenda appear in the James Joyce Quarterly from 1964 onwards.

Slocum, John and Herbert Cahoon. A Bibliography of Joyce (1882-1941). Yale, 1953.

PATRICK KAVANAGH

Kavanagh, Peter. Garden of the Golden Apples. New York, 1973.
48 page bibliography.

Nemo, John. 'A Bibliography of writings by and about Patrick Kavanagh.' Irish University Review 3, no. 1 (spring 1973), pp. 80-106.

J. B. KEANE

See under Fitzmaurice above.

THOMAS KINSELLA

Woodbridge, Hensley C. 'Thomas Kinsella: a bibliography.' Eire-Ireland 2, no. 2 (summer 1967), pp. 122-33.

MARY LAVIN

Doyle, Paul A. 'Mary Lavin: a checklist.' **Papers of the Bibliographical Society of America**, 63 (1969), pp. 317-21.

JOSEPH SHERIDAN LE FANU

Ellis, S.M. 'Bibliography of Joseph Sheridan Le Fanu.' **Irish Book Lover 8**, (1916), pp. 30-3.

Longheed, W.C. 'An Addition to the Le Fanu Bibliography.' **Notes and Queries**, London, 1964

THOMAS D'ARCY McGEE

Coleman, James. 'Bibliography of Thomas D'Arcy McGee.' **Bibliographical Society Ireland 2, no. 7 (1925).**

LOUIS MacNEICE

McKinnon, William T. 'Louis MacNeice: a bibliography.' **Bulletin of Bibliography 27** (1970), pp. 51-52, 48, pp. 79-84.

BRYAN MACMAHON

See under Fitzmaurice above.

M. J. MACMANUS

O'Hegarty, P. S. 'Obituary and bibliography.' **Dublin Magazine**, new series, 27, no. 1 (1952), p. 45.

BRINSLEY MACNAMARA

McDonnell, Michael. 'Brinsley MacNamara, a checklist.' **Journal of Irish Literature 4**, no. 2 (May 1975), pp. 79-88.

JAMES CLARENCE MANGAN

Holzapfel, R.P. **James Clarence Mangan: a check list of printed and other sources. Dublin, 1969.**

Holzapfel, R.P. 'Mangan's poetry in the *Dublin University Magazine:* a bibliography.' **Hermathena** 105 (1967), pp. 40-54.

JOHN MITCHEL

MacManus, M.J. 'Bibliography of the writings of John Mitchel.' **Dublin Magazine**, new series, 16 (1941), pp. 42-50.

GEORGE MOORE

Gilcher, Edwin. **A Bibliography of George Moore.** Illinois, 1970.

THOMAS MOORE

MacManus, M. J. **A Bibliographical hand-list of the first editions of Thomas Moore.** Dublin, 1934.

———. 'A Bibliography of Thomas Moore.' **Dublin Magazine,** new series, 8, no. 2 (1933), pp. 55-61; no. 3, pp. 60-5; no. 4, pp. 56-63; vol. 9, no. 2 (1934), pp. 54-5.

MÁIRTÍN Ó CADHAIN

Titley, Allen. **Máirtín Ó Cadhain: Clár Saothair.** Dublin, 1975.

SEÁN O'CASEY

Black, Hester M. 'A Checklist of first editions of works by Lord Dunsany and Seán O'Casey.' **T.C.D. Annual Bulletin,** 4-8 (1957).

Brandstädter, Otto. 'Ein O'Casey-Bibliographie.' **Zeitschrift fur Anglistik und Amerikanistik.** 2 (1954), pp. 240-54.

Leuidova, I.M. and V. M. Parchevskaia. **Seán O'Casey Bibliographic Guide.** Moscow, 1964.

Mikhail, E.H. **Seán O'Casey: a bibliography of criticism.** London, 1975.

PEADAR O'DONNELL

Doyle, Paul A. 'Peadar O'Donnell: a checklist.' **Bulletin of Bibliography 28,** no. 1 (Jan-March 1971), pp. 3-4.

EIMAR O'DUFFY

MacLochlainn, Alf. 'Eimer O'Duffy: a bibliographical biography.' **Irish Book 1,** no. 2 (1959-60), pp. 37-46.

LIAM O'FLAHERTY

Doyle, Paul A. **Liam O'Flaherty: an annotated bibliography.** New York, 1972.

STANDISH O'GRADY

McKenna, John R. 'The Standish O'Grady collection at Colby College: a checklist.' **Colby Library Quarterly**, series 4, no. 16 (1958), pp. 291-9.

O'Hegarty, P.S. 'Bibliographies of Irish authors, no. 2: Standish O'Grady.' **Dublin Magazine**, new series, 5, no. 2 (1930), pp. 49-56.

SEAMUS O'KELLY

O'Hegarty, P.S. 'Seamus O'Kelly.' **Dublin Magazine**, new series, 9, no. 4 (1934), pp. 47-51.

BRIAN O'NOLAN (Flann O'Brien)

Powell, David. 'A Checklist of Brian O'Nolan.' **Journal of Irish Literature** 3, no. 1 (January 1974), pp. 104-12.

SEUMUS O'SULLIVAN

MacManus, M.J. 'Bibliographies of Irish authors, no. 3: Seumus O'Sullivan.' **Dublin Magazine**, 5, no. 3 (1930), pp. 47-50.

PADRAIC PEARSE

O'Hegarty, P.S. 'P. H. Pearse.' **Dublin Magazine** 6, no. 3 (1931), pp. 44-9.

GEORGE RUSSELL (AE)

Denson, Alan. **Printed writings by George W. Russell (AE): a bibliography.** With some notes on his pictures and portraits. Evanston, Illinois, 1961. Gerrards Cross, Bucks., 1975.

GEORGE BERNARD SHAW

A continuing checklist of Shaviana has been running in the **Shaw Review**, since its inception as the **Shaw Bulletin** in 1951.

Farley, Earl and Marvin Carlson. 'George Bernard Shaw: a selected bibliography (1945-1955).' **Modern Drama** 2 (1959), pp. 188-202, 295-325.

George Bernard Shaw (continued).

Keogh, Lawrence C. 'George Bernard Shaw 1946-1955: a selected bibliography.' **Bulletin of Bibliography** 22 (1959), pp. 224-26; 23 (1960), pp. 20-4, 36-41.

Wells, Geoffrey H. **A Bibliography of the books and pamphlets of George Bernard Shaw.** London, 1928.

ANNA OENONE EDITH SOMERVILLE and MARTIN ROSS

Hudson, Elizabeth. 'A Bibliography of the first editions of the works of E.OE. Somerville and Martin Ross. New York, 1942.

FRANCIS STUART

Natterstad, J.H. 'Francis Stuart: a checklist.' **Journal of Irish Literature** 5, no. 1 (January 1976), pp. 39-45.

J. M. SYNGE

Levitt, Paul M. **J. M. Synge: a bibliography of published criticism.** New York, 1975.

Mikhail, E.H. **J. M. Synge: a bibliography of criticism.** London, 1975.

Pollard, Mary and Ian MacPhail. **John Millington Synge (1871-1909): a catalogue of an exhibition held at Trinity College Library, Dublin.** Dublin, 1959.

JOHN TODHUNTER

'Bibliography.' **Irish Book Lover** 8 (1916-17), pp. 71-2.

MAURICE WALSH

See under Fitzmaurice above.

OSCAR WILDE

Mason, Stuart. **A Bibliography of Wilde.** reprint, London, 1967.

Funke, Peter. **Oscar Wilde in Selbstzeugnissen und bilddokumenten.** Hamburg, 1969.

WILLIAM BUTLER YEATS

Cross, K.G. and R.T. Dunlop. **A Bibliography of Yeats criticism 1887-1965.** London, 1971.
Contains a list of bibliographies, concordances and descriptions of Yeatsiana.

Jochum, K.P.S. **W. B. Yeats: a bibliography of criticism.** Urbana, Illinois, 1976.
Includes a section on the Irish Literary Revival and additions to Allan Wade, *Bibliography of the writings of W.B. Yeats.*

Stoll. John E. **The Great deluge: a Yeats bibliography.** Troy, New York, 1971.

Wade, Allan. **A Bibliography of the writings of William Butler Yeats.** 3rd ed., revised and ed. by Russell K. Alspach. London, 1968.

Literary Periodicals

Introduction

Much of the important work done in a given subject is found in the specialized periodicals. These are quite few in the case of Anglo-Irish literature, but they are important scholarly outlets and contain critical articles, bibliographies and creative writing. Virtually all literary and scholarly journals are likely to have material on Irish literature or about it.

In addition there are periodicals and newspapers in Ireland, even more than have been listed under 'Anglo-Irish literature: literary periodicals' which contain literary, critical or scholarly material. It is one of the trying aspects of Anglo-Irish studies that writers, critics and scholars occasionally publish quite important material in their old school magazine or its equivalent. As a general rule it may be agreed that most of these journals have not been indexed in the general or special periodical indexes or abstracts.

One of the most elusive areas for the research student is that of Irish literary periodicals. While Richard Hayes, *Sources for the history of Irish civilization: articles in Irish periodicals* (1970) has done a great service in indexing periodicals, it is not complete in its coverage and is now going out of date. Unfortunately, most Irish periodicals do not have an index and are not indexed in the standard reference works or in the usual serials. To make a complete bibliography of almost any Irish writer or to get a proper understanding of contemporary issues at any particular period it is however necessary to examine the relevant periodicals.

The following is not a comprehensive list, but a selection of periodicals of literary interest. Since it is virtually impossible to be fully accurate in factual data about dates of publication, number of issues, changing editors, frequency of contribution by particular writers, the list is provided with many reservations, but in the belief that it may nevertheless be useful in pointing towards a rich source of information that is frequently ignored. Obviously all periodicals of this kind ought to be indexed and the task is not impossible.

This list may be supplemented from the *Cambridge bibliography* and the *New Cambridge,* which contain lists of Irish magazines and Irish newspapers, and from the usual sources. See under 'Background: general reference: literature: newspapers and periodicals' and under 'Background: Ireland: newspapers and periodicals: general.'

For the full range of periodicals that have some bearing on literary studies, see the list prefixed to the *M.L.A. international bibliography*. See also Milton Bruce Byrd and Arnold L. Goldsmith, *Publication guide for literary and linguistic scholars* (Wayne State University Studies, humanities, no. 4, Detroit, 1958); Donna Gerstenberger and George Hendrick, *Fourth directory of periodicals publishing articles in English and American literature and language* (Denver, 1975), which is supplemented annually in *Twentieth century literature* and *Ulrich's international periodicals directory,* 13th ed., 2 vols. (New York, 1969).

Acorn, The: a literary magazine. vol. 1, nos. 1-13. Magee University, Northern Ireland, 1961-68.
Contributors: John Hewitt, Sean O'Faolain, W. R. Rodgers.

All-Ireland Review, The: a weekly Irish literary journal. ed. Standish J. O'Grady. vol. 1, no. 1 — vol. 6, no. 52. Kilkenny, 6 Jan. 1900 — Dec. 1906.
Weekly: later irregular. Published much of O'Grady's own work on politics, literature, mythology and the land question.
Contributors: AE., John Eglinton, Maud Gonne, Arthur Griffith, George Moore, John O'Leary, T. W. Rolleston, W. P. Ryan, John Todhunter, W. B. Yeats and several other poets of the Revival.

Arena. eds. Michael Hartnett, James Liddy, Liam O'Connor. nos. 1-4. Coolgreany, Co Wexford, spring 1963 — spring 1965.
Contributors: Austin Clarke, Michael Hartnett, Patrick Kavanagh, Thomas Kinsella, Mary Lavin, James Liddy, Derek Mahon, John Montague, Lorna Reynolds. Indexed in Hayes.

Arrow, The: an occasional publication of the National Theatre Society. ed. W. B. Yeats. vol. 1, nos. 1-5. Dublin, 20 Oct., 1906 — 25 Aug. 1909. Yeats commemoration number, summer, 1939.
Founded, as an arrow of defence, to answer criticism of the National Theatre Society and to explain the principles that motivated Yeats and his associates. The critical writing is all by Yeats and Lady Gregory. Has material on the 'Playboy' controversy.
Contributors to Yeats commemoration number: Austin Clarke, Oliver St John Gogarty, Richard Hayes, F. R. Higgins.
Indexed in Hayes.

Bell, The. ed. Seán O'Faoláin and Peadar O'Donnell. vols. 1-19. Dublin, 1940-54.
The most important periodical of its time; has valuable polemical editorials.
Contributors: Hubert Butler, Austin Clarke, Denis Johnston, Frank O'Connor, Peadar O'Donnell, Seán O'Faoláin, Liam O'Flaherty, and virtually all the contemporary writers.
Indexed in Hayes.

Beltaine: an occasional publication. Organ of the Irish Literary Theatre. ed. W. B. Yeats. Dublin, 1899-1900. (reprint, London, 1970).

The first periodical devoted to the early history and ideas of the Irish dramatic movement; also the first purely literary magazine in Ireland.

Contributors: Lady Gregory, Lionel Johnson, Edward Martyn, Alice Milligan, George Moore, W. B. Yeats.

Blarney Annual. ed. Jos. Reilly. Cork, 1948 - 62.

Contributors: Elizabeth Bowen, Padraic Colum, Mary Lavin, T. C. Murray, Frank O'Connor, Liam O'Flaherty, Seán O'Faoláin, Lennox Robinson.

Capuchin Annual. ed. Father Senan; later Father Henry. Dublin. 1930 —.

Articles on a variety of subjects: literary, religious, art, poetry, plays, fiction, with some creative writing.

Comhar eds. Tomás de Bhalraithe; Proinsias MacCana, Seán MacReamoinn; Máire Mhac an tSaoi; and others. vol. 1 —. Dublin, 1942.

Articles on current affairs, education, language policies, with some creative writing.

Comhthrom Féinne. the college magazine published by the Students' Representative Council of University College, Dublin. no. 1 —. Dublin, 1931-35.

Continued as *The National Student*, 1935 —.

A student publication in which many writers published their early work.

Dana: a magazine of independent thought. ed. John Eglinton and Frederick Ryan. vol. 1. Dublin, May 1904 — April 1905. 12 issues.

Critical of religion, the language revival, the Gaelic League.

Contributors: AE, Padraic Colum, Edward Dowden, John Eglinton, Oliver St John Gogarty, Stephen Gwynn, James Joyce, George Moore, Seumus O'Sullivan, T. W. Rolleston, Fred Ryan, W. B. Yeats.

Dublin Magazine, The. ed. Seumus O'Sullivan. old series, vols. 1-3 (all publ.) Dublin: 1923/24-1925. new series, vols.

Dublin Magazine, The. (continued).

1-33 (all publ.). Dublin, 1926-58.

Monthly then quarterly. Contains many bibliographies.
Contributors: Austin Clarke, George Fitzmaurice, T.C. Murray.
Padraic Fallon, Padraic Colum, Patrick Kavanagh, Samuel
Beckett, Con Leventhal and many others.
An index to contributors to the Dublin Magazine by Rudi
Holzapfel (Dublin, 1966). Indexed also in Hayes.

Dublin Magazine The. ed. Rivers Carew and others. Dublin, 1965-9.

Formerly, *The Dubliner*, 1961- 4.
Contributors: Austin Clarke, Padraic Colum, Monk Gibbon,
Brendan Kennelly, Mary Lavin, Michael Longley, Thomas
MacIntyre, Derek Mahon, Ewart Milne, John Montague, Richard
Murphy, Richard Power.
Indexed in Hayes.

Dublin University Magazine, The: a literary and political journal. vols. 1 - 90. ed. Charles Lever and others. Dublin, 1833-1887.

Continued as *The University Magazine*, a literary and philosophical review. 1878-1879.
See article on *D.U.M. (Ir. Book Lov.* 10, (1918-19) pp. 75-9);
and Michael Sadleir, *Dublin University Magazine: its history,
contents and bibliography (Bibliog. Soc. Ir.* 5, (1933-8). pp.
58-81). Of primary importance. See contributions by Samuel
Ferguson, in particular his review article of Hardiman, *Irish
Minstrelsy*, in four parts, 3 (April, July, Oct, Nov, 1834).

Dublin University Review. Dublin, 1885-1887.

W. B. Yeats was a contributor.
Indexed in Hayes.

Dubliner, The. vols. 1, no. 1 - vol. 3 no. 4. Dublin. 1961-4.

Continued as *The Dublin Magazine*, 1965-9.
Several editors since 1961. Indexed by David Elyan and Rudi
Holzapfel inset to vol. 1 of *The Dublin Magazine*.
Indexed also in Hayes.

Duffy's Fireside Magazine: a monthly miscellany containing original tales and legends. vols. 1-4. Dublin, 1850-4.

Contributors: William Allingham, William Carleton, Gerald
Griffin.

Duffy's Hibernian Magazine: a monthly journal of literature, science and art. Dublin, 1860-4.
3rd series continued as *The Hibernian Magazine.*
Contributors: William Carleton, R. D. Joyce, T. D. McGee, Rev.
C. P. Meehan, John O'Donovan.

Éire-Ireland: a journal of Irish Studies. ed. Eóin McKiernan.
vol. 1, no. 1 —. St. Paul, Minnesota, 1966 —.
Quarterly. vol. 1 no. 1, appeared in March 1966, but mistakenly
bore the date 1965-6.
A valuable inter-disciplinary periodical.

Envoy: a review of literature and art. ed. John Ryan. Poetry
ed. Valentin Iremonger. vol. 1, no. 1 —. Dublin, Dec. 1949-51.
[20 nos. all published].
A critical journal. European outlook; Irish material; reproduction
of paintings.
Contributors: Brendan Behan, Denis Devlin, John Hewitt, Valentin Iremonger, Patrick Kavanagh, Mary Lavin, Seán Ó'Faoláin,
Brian O'Nolan, Francis Stuart.
Indexed in Hayes.

Feasta. ed. Seosamh Ó Duibhginn. vol. 1 —. Dublin, 1948.
Encouraged new Irish writing.

Green and Gold: a magazine of fiction, etc. ed Alan Downey.
Waterford, 1924-6.
Contributors: Padraic Colum, Brinsley MacNamara, James
Stephens, Katharine Tynan.
Indexed in Hayes.

Green Sheaf, The. ed. Pamela Coleman Smith. nos. 1-13
(all publ). London, 1903-4.
Contributors: AE, Lady Gregory, John M. Synge, John Todhunter,
W. B. Yeats. One of its main topics: dreams. Illustrated in colour
and black and white by Gordon Craig, Colman Smith and others.

Hibernian Magazine, The. See **Duffy's Hibernian Magazine**
above.

Holy Door, The. ed. Brian Lynch. Dublin, summer 1965 —
spring 1966.
Contributors: Michael Hartnett, Pearse Hutchinson, Patrick
Kavanagh, Anthony Kerrigan, Thomas Kinsella, Ewart Milne,
John Montague, Desmond O'Grady.

Honest Ulsterman, The. ed. James Simmons to May 1969, then by Michael Foley and Frank Ormsby. no. 1 –. Portrush, May 1968 –.

Contributors: Seamus Heaney, John Hewitt, Brendan Kennelly, Michael Longley, John McGahern, Derek Mahon, James Simmons and most contemporary writers.

Ireland Today. ed. Michael O'Donovan [Frank O'Connor]. Dublin, June 1936 – March 1938. [22 issues publ.].

Monthly.
Contributors: Brian Coffey, Daniel Corkery, Denis Devlin, Michael MacLaverty, Ewart Milne, Frank O'Connor, Seán O'Faoláin, Liam O'Flaherty, Mervyn Wall.
Indexed in Hayes.

Irish Book, The. ed. Alf MacLochlainn. vol. 1, no. 1 - vol. 3, no. 1. Dublin, 1959 - 1964.

No more published.

Irish Book Lover, The: a monthly review of Irish literature and bibliography. ed. John S. Crone; later Seamus Ó Casaide; then Colm O'Lochlainn. vol. 1, no. 1 – vol. 32, no. 6. London, 1909-57.

Monthly.
Subjects: topography, bibliography, reviews, literary events and information.
Contributors: F. R. McC. Dix, John S. Crone.
Index to vols. 1-31 (1909-51), compiled by Eugene Carberry, in typescript in the National Library, Dublin.

Irish Booklore. vol. 1 (1970); vol. 2 (1976) –. Belfast.

Irish Bookman, The. ed. Seamus Campbell. vol. 1, no. 1 –. Dublin, 1946-8.

Materials: creative work, reviews, book notes.
Contributors: Pearse Hutchinson, Thomas MacGreevy, Michael MacLaverty, James Plunkett.

Irish Monthly, The. ed. Rev. Matthew Russell, S.J. 83 vols. Dublin, 1873 - 1954.

A semi-religious magazine. Contains early work by many poets including Yeats.
Contributors: Alice Curtayne, Robert Farren, Maurice Leahy, Francis McManus, Katharine Tynan.
Indexed in Hayes.

Irish Penny Journal, The. ed. George Petrie. vol. 1. Dublin, 1840-1.

Contributors: William Carleton, James Clarence Mangan, John O'Donovan, Edward Walsh.

Irish Review, The: a monthly magazine of Irish literature, art and science. ed. David Houston, 1911-12; Padraic Colum, 1912-13; Joseph Plunkett, 1913-14; associate editor, Thomas McDonagh, 1911-14. Dublin, 1911-14.

Monthly. Primarily a literary journal, with a sensible policy. Published poetry, fiction, drama, criticism.
Contributors: every major writer from Standish James O'Grady to Padraic Pearse. AE, Ernest Boyd, Joseph Campbell, Roger Casement, Padraic Colum, Daniel Corkery, Lord Dunsany, John Eglinton, Oliver St John Gogarty, Maud Gonne, Arthur Griffith, Douglas Hyde, Thomas Kettle, Thomas MacDonagh, George Moore, Eimar O'Duffy, Seumus O'Sullivan, Padraic Pearse, Joseph Mary Plunkett, Forrest Reid, Fred Ryan, James Stephens, Katharine Tynan, Jack B. Yeats, John B. Yeats, W. B. Yeats
Author, title and general subject index in each vol.
Indexed also in Hayes.

Irish Statesman, The. ed. G. W. Russell (AE). Dublin, 1919-30.

Formerly *The Irish Homestead*. Published most of the important writers, See Edward Doyle Smith, *The Irish statesman: a survey and index* (1923-1930), (Ann Arbor, 1966).

Irish University Review: a journal of Irish studies. ed. Maurice Harmon. vol. 1 —. Dublin, 1970 —.

An inter-disciplinary critical journal.
Contributors: Austin Clarke, Brian Coffey, Seamus Heaney, John Montague, Richard Murphy, Seán Ó'Faoláin.
Publishes IASAIL's annual 'Bibliography Bulletin'.
Formerly *University Review*, 1955-68.

Irish Writing: the magazine of contemporary Irish literature. ed. David Marcus and Terence Smith, 1946-54; Seán J. White, Dec. 1954-57. Cork, 1946-57.

37 issues. Quarterly.
Poetry, fiction, plays, criticism, reviews.
Contributors: Teresa Deevy, Robert Greacen, Patrick Kavanagh, John Montague, Frank O'Connor, Seán Ó'Faoláin, Liam O'Flaherty.
Indexed in Hayes.

Irisleabhar Mha Nuat. vol. 1 —. Maynooth, 1907.
Since 1967 has developed as a journal of literary criticism.

James Joyce Quarterly. vol. 1, no. 1—. Tulsa, Oklahoma, 1963 —.
See also *A Wake Newsletter*, vol. 1, no. 1 —, (Essex, 1964 —).

Journal of Irish Literature. ed. Robert Hogan. vol. 1, no. 1 —.
Newark, Delaware, 1972 —.
Published three times a year, in January, May and September.

Journal of National Literary Society of Ireland. vol. 1, no. 1 —
vol. 2. Dublin, 1892 - 1916.
Irregular. vol. 1 (1892-1904); vol. 2 (1904-16).
A record of lectures given by the Society, founded by Yeats and
others; bibliography of lectures given. Lectures by Douglas Hyde,
Lionel Johnson, Alfred Nutt, Eugene O'Curry, John O'Leary,
George Sigerson, W. B. Yeats.
Subjects: literature, music, language, art, politics, old Irish law.
Indexed in Hayes.

Kavanagh's Weekly. ed. Patrick Kavanagh. nos. 1-13. Dublin,
12 April 1952 — 5 July 1952.
Contributors: Brendan Behan, Myles na gCopaleen, Joseph Hone,
Patrick Kavanagh.

Kilkenny Magazine. ed. James Delehanty. Kilkenny, 1960 —.
Contributors: John Banville, Padraic Colum, Monk Gibbon,
Pearse Hutchinson, Patrick Kavanagh, Thomas Kinsella, Ewart
Milne, John Montague, Frank O'Connor, Desmond O'Grady.
Indexed in Hayes.

Lace Curtain, The: a magazine of poetry and criticism. ed.
Michael Smith. no. 1 —. Dublin, autumn, 1969 —.
Contributors: Brian Coffey, Patrick Galvin, Anthony Kerrigan,
Thomas Kinsella, Niall Montgomery, Michael Smith.
No. 4 (summer, 1971) a valuable issue on the Thirties, with con-
tributions from Samuel Beckett, Austin Clarke, Brian Coffey,
Denis Devlin, Arthur Power, George Reavey, Mervyn Wall.

Long Room: an illustrated journal devoted to Irish bibliographical studies. vol. 1 —. Dublin, 1970 —.

Lyceum, The: a monthly educational and literary magazine.
ed. Father Thomas Finlay (1887-8); and William Magennis
(1887-94). Dublin, 1887-94.
Continued as *The New Ireland Review*.
Interested in history, education, economics, politics, literature.

Macaomh, An. ed. P.H. Pearse. Dublin, 1909-13.
Only four numbers published.
Contributors: Joseph Campbell, Padraic Colum, Padraic Pearse,
Thomas MacDonagh. Illustrated by AE, Jack Yeats.
Indexed in Hayes.

Motley: the Dublin Gate Theatre magazine. ed. Mary
Manning. nos. 1-19. Dublin, March 1932 — May 1934.
Contributors: Austin Clarke, Michael MacLiammoir, Mary
Manning, Seán O'Faoláin.

Nation, The. ed Thomas Davis. vol. 1 — vol. 10. Dublin,
1846-96.
Contributors included most contemporary writers including
Thomas Davis, Douglas Hyde, James Clarence Mangan, John
Mitchel.

National Student, The. Dublin, 1910-21; 1930-52.
Formerly *Comhthrom Féinne*, 1931-5. See above.

**New Ireland Review The: a monthly educational and literary
magazine.** ed. Father Thomas Finlay, vol, 1 — 34. 8 vols.
Dublin, 1894 - 1911.
Formerly *The Lyceum* (1887-94).
Promoted serious and enlightened discussion. Maintained same
wide interests as its predecessor, but had special interest in history
and literature.
Contributors: AE, James Cousins, W. H. Grattan-Flood, Eleanor
Hull, Douglas Hyde, *(Religious songs of Connacht)*, Thomas
Kettle, Eoin MacNeill, George Moore, Moira O'Neill, Horace
Plunkett, T. W. Rolleston, Fred Ryan, George Sigerson, J. M.
Synge, John Todhunter, W. B. Yeats.

Non-Plus. ed. Patricia Avis. nos. 1-4 (all publ). Dublin,
1959-60.
Quarterly.
Contributors: Myles na gCopaleen, Patrick Kavanagh, Ewart
Milne, T. de Vere White.

Poetry Ireland. (Supplement to *Irish Writing*). ed. David
Marcus. nos. 1-28. Dublin, 1948-55.
Quarterly.
An all poetry magazine.
Contributors: Austin Clarke, Patrick Kavanagh, Thomas Kinsella,
Ewart Milne, John Montague, W. R. Rodgers.
Indexed in Hayes.

Poetry Ireland. ed. John Jordan. no. 1 —. (8 issues). Dublin, 1962-8.

Irregular.

An attempt to find an Irish audience.

Contributors: Austin Clarke, Brian Coffey, Seamus Heaney, John Jordan, Patrick Kavanagh, Thomas Kinsella, Derek Mahon, John Montague.

St Stephen's: a record of university life, 1900-1905. eds. Hugh Kennedy, Felix Hackett, C.P. Curran, John Kennedy, Cruise O'Brien. Dublin 1901-6.

Contains the early work of James Joyce, Thomas Kettle, Padraic Pearse, F. Sheehy-Skeffington; also George O'Neill, Canon Sheehan, George Sigerson.

———. new series, 1930 —.

———. series 2, 1960-71.

Series of writers on writing.

———. vol. 3, 1974 —.

Samhain: an occasional publication. Organ of the National Theatre Society. ed. W. B. Yeats. Dublin and London, 1901-5, 1908. (reprint, London, 1970).

Six issues, Oct. 1901-5; one issue, Nov. 1908.

Annual.

Succeeded *Beltaine*.

Subjects: creative material and literary articles.

Contains much drama criticism and several one-act plays by Lady Gregory, Douglas Hyde, J. M. Synge, W. B. Yeats and others.

Contributors: AE, Lady Gregory, Robert Gregory, Douglas Hyde, George Moore, J. M. Synge, Jack Yeats, W. B. Yeats.

Yeats's essays have been reprinted in *Explorations*.

Indexed in Hayes.

Shan Van Vocht, The. ed. Ethna Carbery and Alice Milligan. Belfast, 1896-9.

Nationalistic and literary.

Studies: an Irish quarterly review. vol. 1 —. Dublin, 1912 —.

An interdisciplinary journal. Occasional articles by Irish writers.

General index of volumes 1-50, 1912-1961, compiled by Aloysius O'Rahilly (Ros Cré, 1966).

Indexed also in Hayes.

Threshold. ed. Mary O'Malley. Poetry ed. John Hewitt. vol. 1, no. 1—. Belfast, spring 1957 —.
Quarterly, then bi-annually.
Since vol. 5 no. 2, has had several guest eds: John Boyd, Brian Friel, Patrick Galvin, Seamus Heaney, John Montague.
Subject matter: poetry, short fiction, literary criticism.
Contributors: Austin Clarke, Brian Coffey, Padraic Colum, Brian Friel, Seamus Heaney, John Hewitt, Patrick Kavanagh, Thomas Kinsella, Derek Mahon, John Montague, Frank O'Connor.
Vol. 1 —. (1957-69).
Indexed in Hayes.

To-Morrow. ed. Lawrence K. Emery (Dr A. J. Leventhal). 2 issues: Aug., Sept., 1924. Dublin, 1924.
Contributors: Joseph Campbell, F. R. Higgins, Liam O'Flaherty, Cecil Ffrench Salkeld, Francis Stuart, W. B. Yeats.

Uladh: a literary and critical magazine. ed. Bulmer Hobson and Joseph Campbell. nos. 1-4. Belfast, Nov. 1904 — Sept. 1905.
Set out to be the organ of the Ulster Literary Theatre.
Contributors: AE, Joseph Campbell, Roger Casement, Padraic Colum, Stephen Gwynn, Bulmer Hobson, Herbert Hughes, Alice Milligan, Forrest Reid.
Indexed in Hayes.

Ulster Review, The: a progressive monthly of individuality. ed. A. S. Moore. Belfast, 1924-26.
Contributors: Lynn Doyle, Stephen Gwynn, Shane Leslie, Forrest Reid.

United Irishman, The: a national weekly review. ed Arthur Griffith. Dublin, 1899-1906.
Contributors: AE, John Eglinton, Frank Fay, Arthur Griffith, Douglas Hyde, Edward Martyn, Alice Milligan, P. S. O'Hegarty, Seumus O'Sullivan, Padraic Pearse, T. W. Rolleston, J. B. Yeats, W. B. Yeats.

University Magazine, The: a literary and philosophical review. vol. 1-4. Dublin, 1878-9.
Formerly the *Dublin University Magazine*, q.v.

University Review. ed. Lorna Reynolds. The organ of the Graduates Association of the National University of Ireland. Dublin, 1954-68.

Quarterly. Continued as the *Irish University Review*.

Contributors: Austin Clarke, Pearse Hutchinson, Thomas Kinsella, Kate O'Brien.

Chronology

Ireland   England, Europe, America, etc.

1765 Thomas Percy. *Reliques of
ancient English poetry.*
1765 Oliver Goldsmith. *The Vicar of
Wakefield.*
1779 Samuel Johnson. *Lives of the
poets* (1779-81).

1789 Charlotte Brooke, *Reliques
of Irish poetry.*

1789 Robert Burns, *Poems.*
William Blake. *Songs of inno-
cence.*
1790 Edmund Burke. *Reflections
on the French Revolution.*
1791 Thomas Paine. *Rights of man,*
(1791-2).
James Boswell. *Life of Johnson.*

1793 William Godwin. *Inquiry con-
cerning political justice.*

1794 William Blake. *Songs of experience.*
Thomas Paine. *The Age of
reason.*
1795 Johann W. von Goethe. *Wilhelm
Meisters Lehrjahre.*

1796 Edward Bunting. *Ancient
Irish music.*

1798 Samuel Taylor Coleridge and
William Wordsworth. *Lyrical
Ballads.*

England, Europe, America, etc.   Ireland

                                        1738 d. of Turlough O'Carolan.

                                        1781 The Custom House built
                                              (1781-91); designed by James
                                              Gandon.
1782 American Revolution in   1782 Grattan's Parliament.
      progress.
1784 d. of Samuel Johnson.   1784 d. of Eoghan Ruadh
                                              O'Suilleabhain.
                                        1785 Royal Irish Academy, Dublin,
                                              founded.
                                        1786 Building of the Four Courts
                                              (1786-96); designed by James
                                              Gandon.

1788 Trial of Warren Hastings.
      b. of Lord Byron.
1789 French Revolution.

                                        1791 Founding of United Irishmen.

                                        1792 Harp Festival in Belfast.
1793 Louis XVI and Marie   1793 Relaxation of Penal Laws.
      Antoinette executed. Reign
      of Terror begins in France.
      War between Britain and
      France.

                                        1794 b. of William Carleton.

                                        1795 Maynooth founded.
                                              The Orange Order founded.
1796 d. of Robert Burns and James   1796 Wolfe Tone's attempted in-
      Macpherson.   vasion.
                                        1798 Rising of the United Irishmen.
                                              d. of Wolfe Tone.

Ireland

England, Europe, America, etc.

Charles B. Brown. *Wieland, or
the transformation.*
Thomas Malthus. *Essay on the
principle of population.*
1800 Maria Edgeworth. *Castle Rackrent.* 1800 Mme. de Staël. *On literature.*

1802 *Edinburgh Review.*

1804 Johann Christoph Friedrich von
Schiller. *Wilhelm Tell.*
1805 Sir Walter Scott. *Lay of the last
minstrel.*
1806 Lady Morgan. *The Wild Irish girl.*
1808 John Philpot Curran. *Speeches.*
Thomas Moore. *Irish Melodies* (1808-34).
1809 Maria Edgeworth. *Tales of fashion-* 1809 *Quarterly Review.*
able life (1809-12). Washington Irving. *Rip van Winkle.*
August W. von Schlegel. *Lectures
on dramatic art and literature.*
1810 Sir Walter Scott. *The Lady of the
lake.*
1811 Jane Austen. *Sense and sensibility.*
Johann W. von Goethe. *Aus Meinem
leben, dichtung und warheit (1811-33).*
1812 Lord Byron. *Childe Harold's
pilgrimage.*

1813 Jane Austen. *Pride and prejudice.*
Robert Owen. *A New view of
society.*
1814 Sir Walter Scott. *Waverley.*

1816 Jane Austen. *Emma.*
Blackwood's Magazine founded in
Edinburgh.
1817 Thomas Moore. *Lalla Rookh.* 1817 Sir Samuel Taylor Coleridge.
Maria Edgeworth. *Ormond.* *Biographia literaria.*
Lord Byron. *Manfred.*
1818 Lord Byron. *Don Juan.*
Mary W. Shelley. *Frankenstein.*

England, Europe, America, etc.   Ireland

1800 Act of Union between Britain
and Ireland.

1802 Peace of Amiens between Britain   1802 First Christian Brothers School
and France.   opened.

1803 Rising of Robert Emmet.
d. of James Malton, draftsman.

1805 d. of Brian Merriman.
Grattan makes maiden speech
in U.K. Parliament.

1808 b. of Michael Balfe, composer,
(1808-70).

1810 Napoleon at the height of power.

1811 The Regency (1811-20).

1812 b. of Vincent Wallace, composer,
(1812-65).
d. of Edward Smyth, sculptor,
(1749-1812).

1814 Congress of Vienna.
British force burns Washington, D.C.

1815 Defeat of Napoleon at Waterloo.
Corn Law passed in England.

1817 d. of Jane Austen.
Erie Canal being built.

Ireland	England, Europe, America, etc.
	1819 Percy Bysshe Shelley. *Masque of anarchy.* John Keats writes his great Odes.
1820 Charles Robert Maturin. *Melmoth the wanderer.*	1820 *London Magazine.* Sir Walter Scott. *Ivanhoe.*
	1821 Percy Bysshe Shelley. *Adonais.* Sir Walter Scott. *Kenilworth.*
1824 Thomas Crofton Croker. *Researches in the South of Ireland.*	1824 *Westminster Review.*
1825 John Banim. *Croohore of the Billhook. Christian Examiner* begins.	1825 William Hazlitt. *The Spirit of the age.*
1826 John and Michael Banim. *The Boyne Water.*	1826 James Fenimore Cooper. *The Last of the Mohicans.*
1827 Lady Morgan. *The O'Briens and the O'Flahertys.*	
1829 T. Crofton Croker. *Legends of the lakes.* Gerald Griffin. *The Collegians.*	1829 Honoré de Balzac. *La Comédie humaine* (1829-48).
1830 William Carleton. *Traits and stories of the Irish peasantry.* (1830-33).	1830 Stendhal. *La Rouge et la noir.*
1831 James Hardiman. *Irish minstrelsy.*	1831 Edgar Allan Poe. *Poems.*
1832 *Dublin Penny Journal* begins.	1832 Lord Alfred Tennyson. *The Lady of Shalott* and *Morte d'Arthur.*
1833 *Dublin University Magazine,* founded by Isaac Butt and others.	1833 Honoré de Balzac. *Eugénie Grandet.* Robert Browning. *Pauline.*
	1834 Honoré de Balzac. *Le Père Goriot.* Victor Hugo. *The Hunchback of Notre Dame.*
1835 George Darley. *Nepenthe.*	
	1836 Charles Dickens. *Sketches by Boz. Pickwick papers (1836-37).* Ralph Waldo Emerson. *Nature.* Nikolai Gogol. *The Government inspector.* Alfred de Musset. *Confessions d'un enfant du siècle.*
	1837 Thomas Carlyle. *The French Revolution.* Nathaniel Hawthorne. *Twice-told tales.*

England, Europe, America, etc.	Ireland
1819 The 'Peterloo Massacre'.	
1820 Accession of George IV.	1820 d. of Henry Grattan.
1821 d. of Napoleon and John Keats.	1821 Theatre Royal, Dublin, opens.
1822 d. of Percy Bysshe Shelley.	
	1823 d. of James Gandon, architect, (1743-1823).
1824 Election of John Quincy Adams. d. of Lord Byron.	
1827 d. of William Blake.	
	1829 Catholic Emancipation.
	1831 National School system established.
1832 The Reform Bill carried in Parliament. d. of Sir Walter Scott.	
1834 d. of Samuel Taylor Coleridge.	
	1835 d. of Anthony Raftery.
1836 Davy Crockett killed at the Alamo.	
1837 Accession of Queen Victoria.	

Ireland	England, Europe, America, etc.
	1838 Charles Dickens. *Oliver Twist.* *Nicholas Nickleby* (1838-39). Thomas Carlyle. *Sartor Resartus.*
1839 Charles Lever. *Harry Lorrequer.* William Carleton. *Fardorougha, the miser.*	1839 Edgar Allan Poe. *The Fall of the house of Usher.* Stendhal. *La Chartreuse de Parme.*
	1841 Thomas Carlyle. *On heroes, hero worship, and the heroic in history.*
1842 *The Nation* founded. Samuel Lover. *Handy Andy.*	1842 Henry Wadsworth Longfellow. *Poems of slavery.* Thomas Babington Macaulay. *Lays of Ancient Rome.*
	1843 Thomas Carlyle. *Past and Present.* W. H. Prescott. *History of the conquest of Mexico.* Lord Alfred Tennyson. *Morte d'Arthur; Locksley hall.* John Ruskin. *Modern painters.*
	1844 Alexandre Dumas. *Le Comte de Monte Cristo.* Heinrich Heine. *Neue gedichte.* William Makepeace Thackeray. *Barry Lyndon.*
1845 George Petrie. *The Ecclesiastical architecture of Ireland.* James Clarence Mangan. *Anthologia Germanica.* J. Sheridan Le Fanu. *The Cock and anchor.* William Carleton. *Valentine McClutchy, the Irish agent.* Sir Charles Gavan Duffy. *The Ballad-poetry of Ireland.*	1845 Prosper Mérimée. *Carmen.*
1846 Thomas Davis. *Poems* and *Literary essays.*	1846 Fëdor M. Dostoevski. *Poor folk.* Herman Melville. *Typee.*
1847 William Carleton. *The Black prophet.* Charles Lever. *The Martins of Cro' Martin* and *The Knight of Gwynne.*	1847 Emily Bronte. *Wuthering Heights.* Charlotte Bronte. *Jane Eyre.* William Makepeace Thackeray. *Vanity fair.*
1848 John Mitchel founds *United Irishman.* John O'Donovan. *Annals of the Four Masters* (1848-51). William Carleton. *The Emigrants of Ahadarra.*	1848 Karl Marx and Friedrich Engles. *Communist manifesto.* John Stuart Mill. *Principles of political economy.*
1849 John O'Daly. *The Poets and poetry of Munster.*	1849 Charles Dickens. *David Copperfield.*

England, Europe, America, etc.   Ireland

1839   b. of John Butler Yeats
       (1839-1922).

1842   d. of Stendhal.   1842   O'Connell calls off monster meet-
                                               ing at Clontarf.

1843   Wordsworth appointed English
       poet laureate.

1844   Meeting of Marx and Engles in
       Paris.

1845   d. of Andrew Jackson.   1845   d. of Thomas Davis.
                                               b. of Standish O'Grady.

1846   Repeal of Corn Laws.   1846   The Great Famine (1846-48).

1847   First gold rush to California.   1847   d. of Daniel O'Connell.

1848   End of American-Mexican war.   1848   Rising of the Young Irelanders.
       Revolt in Paris and Rome.
       Revolution in Vienna and Venice.
       Founding of Pre-Raphaelite Brother-
       hood.
1849   d. of Edgar Allan Poe.   1849   d. of Maria Edgeworth.
                                               d. of James Clarence Mangan.

Ireland   England, Europe, America, etc.

1850 Lord Alfred Tennyson. *In memoriam.*
      Elizabeth Barrett Browning. *Sonnets
      from the Portuguese.*
      Nathaniel Hawthorne. *The Scarlet
      letter.*
      Ralph Waldo Emerson. *Represent-
      ative man.*

1851 Nathaniel Hawthorne. *The House
      of the seven gables.*
      Herman Melville. *Moby Dick.*
      John Ruskin. *Stones of Venice.*

1852 William Makepeace Thackeray. *The
      History of Henry Esmond.*
      Charles Dickens. *Bleak House.*
      Théophile Gautier. *Émaux et camees*
      (1850-65).
      Ivan Turgenev. *A Sportsman's sketches.*

1853 Matthew Arnold. *The Scholar gipsy.*
      Nathaniel Hawthorne. *Tanglewood
      tales.*

1854 John Mitchel. *Jail journal.*   1854 Henry Thoreau. *Walden, or life in the
                                                  woods.*

1855 Anthony Trollope. *The Warden.*
      Walt Whitman. *Leaves of grass.*
      Robert Browning. *Men and women.*
      Henry Wadsworth Longfellow. *The
      Song of Hiawatha.*
      Lord Alfred Tennyson. *Maud.*
      Herbert Spencer. *Principles of psy-
      chology.*

1856 Gustave Flaubert. *Madame Bovary.*

1857 Charles Baudelaire. *Les Fleurs du mal.*
      Anthony Trollope. *Barchester Towers.*
      Thomas Huxley. *The Theory of the
      vertebrate skulls.*

1858 William Morris. *The Defence of
      Guenevere.*

1859 Charles Darwin. *The Origin of species
      by means of natural selection.*
      Lord Alfred Tennyson. *Idylls of the
      king.*

England, Europe, America, etc.	Ireland
1850 d. of Honoré de Balzac and William Wordsworth. Lord Alfred Tennyson becomes poet laureate.	1850 Tenant League founded. Appointment of Archbishop Cullen.
1851 The Great Exhibition in London.	
	1852 b. of Lady Gregory and George Moore. d. of Thomas Moore.
	1853 Formation of Ossianic Society.
1854 Siege of Sebastapol.	1854 Catholic University of Ireland founded, with John Henry (later Cardinal) Newman as rector.
1856 Anglo-Chinese war begins.	1856 James Stephens returns to Ireland from Paris. b. of George Bernard Shaw and Oscar Wilde.
1857 Garibaldi forms Italian Association for unification of the country.	
	1858 Fenian movement founded. d. of John Hogan, sculptor, (1800-1858).

Ireland	England, Europe, America, etc.
	John Stuart Mill. *Essay on liberty.*
	George Eliot. *Adam Bede.*
1860 Dion Boucicault. *The Colleen bawn.* John Mitchel. *The last conquest of Ireland (perhaps).*	1860 Charles Dickens. *Great Expectations* (1860-61). Wilkie Collins. *The Woman in white.* George Eliot. *The Mill on the floss.*
1861 Eugene O'Curry. *Manuscript materials of ancient Irish history.*	
	1862 Ivan Turgenev. *Fathers and sons.* Gustave Flaubert. *Salammbo.* Victor Hugo. *Les Misérables.*
1863 *The Irish People.* Joseph Sheridan Le Fanu. *The House by the churchyard.*	1863 John Stuart Mill. *Utilitarianism.* J. E. Renan. *La Vie de Jésus: Histoire des origines du Christianisme.*
1864 William Allingham. *Laurence Bloomfield in Ireland.* Joseph Sheridan Le Fanu. *Uncle Silas.*	1864 L. Tolstoy. *War and peace.* Cardinal J. H. Newman. *Apologia pro vita sua.*
1865 Sir Samuel Ferguson. *Lays of the western gael.*	1865 Matthew Arnold. *Essays in criticism.* A. C. Swinburne. *Atlanta in Calydon.* Mark Twain. *The Jumping frog of Calaveras county.* Walt Whitman. *Drum-taps.*
	1866 A. C. Swinburne. *Poems and ballads.* Paul Verlaine. *Poèmes Saturniens.* Charles Baudelaire. *Les Epauls.* Alphonse Daudet. *Lettres de mon moulin.* Fëdor M. Dostoevski. *Crime and punishment.* Henrik Ibsen. *Brand.*
	1867 Anthony Trollope. *The Last chronicle of Barset.* Émile Zola. *Thérèse Raquin.* Henrik Ibsen. *Peer Gynt.* Karl Marx. *Das Kapital.*
	1868 Robert Browning. *The Ring and the book.* Fëdor M. Dostoevski. *The Idiot.*
	1869 Matthew Arnold. *Culture and anarchy.* Gustave Flaubert. *L'Éducation sentimentale.* Mark Twain. *Innocents abroad.* Paul Verlaine. *Fêtes galantes.*

England, Europe, America, etc.   Ireland

1860   Election of Abraham Lincoln.
       The Cornhill Magazine founded.
       Garibaldi enters Naples.

1861   American Civil War begins.   1861   Funeral of Terence Bellew
                                                MacManus.
1862   Bismarck becomes Prime Minister
       of Prussia.

1863   Gettysburg.
       d. of William Makepeace Thackeray.
       Revolt in Poland.
1864   General Sherman marches through
       Georgia.
       Abraham Lincoln re-elected.
       d. of Nathaniel Hawthorne.
1865   Abraham Lincoln assassinated.   1865   b. of William Butler Yeats.
       End of Civil War.   J. O'Donovan (Rossa), and John
       d. of William Hamilton.   O'Leary sentenced.

1866   Fenian raids on Canada.   1866   Arrest and escape of James
                                                Stephens.

1867   Garibaldi marches on Rome.   1867   Fenian Rising.
       d. of Charles Baudelaire.   Manchester Martyrs.
                                                b. of George Russell (AE.).

1868   Benjamin Disraeli becomes Prime
       Minister.
       William E. Gladstone becomes
       Prime Minister.

                                         1869   Dis-establishment of the Church
                                                of Ireland.
                                                d. of William Carleton.

		1871	George Eliot. *Middlemarch.*
			Charles Darwin. *The Descent of man.*
			Emile Zola. *Les Rougon Macquart* (1871-93).
			Algernon Charles Swinburne. *Songs before sunrise.*
1872	Sir Samuel Ferguson. *Congal.*	1872	Samuel Butler. *Erewhon, or over the range.*
			Thomas Hardy. *Under the greenwood tree.*
1873	Eugene O'Curry. *Manners and customs of the ancient Irish.* P. W. Joyce. *Ancient Irish music.*	1873	Arthur Rimbaud. *Une Saison en enfer.* L. Tolstoy. *Anna Karenina.* Walter Pater. *Studies in the history of the renaissance.* Matthew Arnold. *Literature and dogma.*
		1874	Gustave Flaubert. *La Tentation de Saint Antoine.* Paul Verlaine. *Romances sans paroles.* Arthur Rimbaud. *Les Illuminations.*
		1875	Mark Twain. *The Adventures of Tom Sawyer.* Stéphane Mallarmé. *L'Après-midi d'un faune.*
		1876	Henry James. *Roderick Hudson.*
		1877	Henrik Ibsen. *The Pillars of society.* Henry James. *The American.* Émile Zola. *L'Assommoir.*
1878	Standish O'Grady. *Bardic history of Ireland.*	1878	Thomas Hardy. *The Return of the native.* A. C. Swinburne. *Poems and ballads.*
1879	Charles Kickham. *Knocknagow.*	1879	Henrik Ibsen. *A Doll's house.* Henry James. *Daisy Miller.* George Meredith. *The Egoist.* Robert Louis Stevenson. *Travels with a donkey.* August Strindberg. *The Red room.*

England, Europe, America, etc.

1870 Franco-Prussian war.
       d. of Charles Dickens.
       Heinrich Schliemann begins to
       excavate Troy.
       Dogma of Papal infallibility.
       d. of General Robert E. Lee.
       The Education Act.

Ireland

1870 Gladstone's first land Act.
       Isaac Butt begins Home Rule
       movement.
       Michael Davitt sentenced to 15
       years' penal servitude.
       d. of Daniel MacLise, painter,
       (1806-1870).

1871 b. of John Millington Synge and
       Jack Butler Yeats.

1872 Civil war in Spain.
       d. of Giuseppe Mazzini.

1873 Republic declared in Spain.

1874 First impressionist exhibition in
       Paris.
       Benjamin Disraeli Prime Minister.

1874 d. of Henry Foley, sculptor,
       (1818-1874).

1875 Theosophical Society founded by
       Helena Blavatsky.

1875 Charles Stewart Parnell elected to
       Parliament.

1876 Invention of the telephone.
1877 Invention of the phonograph.

1877 Release of Michael Davitt.

1878 Manufacture of first bicycles in
       America.
       Paris World Exhibition.

1878 b. of Daniel Corkery.
       d. of Cardinal Cullen.

1879 Beginning of the Land League,
       founded by Michael Davitt with
       Charles Stewart Parnell as pres-
       ident, and of the 'land war'.
       d. of Isaac Butt.

Ireland	England, Europe, America, etc.

1880 Standish O'Grady. *History of Ireland: Cuchulainn and his contemporaries.*
Joseph Sheridan Le Fanu. *The Parnell papers.*

1880 Fëdor M. Dostoevski. *The Brothers Karamazov.*
Guy de Maupassant. *Contes* (1880-90).
Émile Zola. *Nana.*

1881 Gustave Flaubert. *Bouvard et Pécuchet.*
Henry James. *Portrait of a lady.*
Paul Verlaine. *Sagesse.*

1882 *The Gaelic Journal.*

1882 Robert Louis Stevenson. *Treasure island.*
Henrik Ibsen. *An Enemy of the people.*

1883 Guy de Maupassant. *Une Vie.*
F. W. Nietzsche. *Also sprach Zarathustra.*

1884 Mark Twain. *Huckleberry Finn.*
Paul Verlaine. *Jadis et Naguère.*
Henrik Ibsen. *The Wild duck.*
J. C. Huysmans. *A Rebours.*

1885 Walter Pater. *Marius the epicurean.*
Émile Zola. *Germinal.*
William D. Howells. *The Rise of Silas Lapham.*

1886 George Moore. *A Drama in Muslin.*
John O'Leary. *What Irishmen should know.*

1886 Henry James. *The Bostonians.*
Pierre Loti. *Pêcheur d'Islande.*
Robert Louis Stevenson. *Dr Jekyll and Mr Hyde.*
Henrik Ibsen. *Rosmersholm.*
Karl Marx. *Das Kapital* published in London.
Richard von Krafft-Ebing. *Psychopathia sexualis.*

1887 August Strindberg. *The Father.*
Stephane Mallarmé. *Poésies.*

1888 *Poems and ballads of Young Ireland.*
1889 W. B. Yeats. *The Wanderings of Oisin.*
1890 Douglas Hyde. *Beside the fire.*

1888 Guy de Maupassant. *Pierre et Jean.*
1889 Walter Pater. *Appreciations.*
Thomas Huxley. *Agnosticism.*
1890 L. Tolstoy. *The Kreutzer sonata.*
Henrik Ibsen. *Hedda Gabler.*
Oscar Wilde. *The Picture of Dorian Gray.*

England, Europe, America, etc.   **Ireland**

1880   William E. Gladstone becomes Prime
       Minister.
       d. of Gustave Flaubert and George
       Eliot.
       First practical electric lights devised.
1881   d. of Fëdor M. Dostoevski.

1880   b. of Seán O'Casey.
       St. Stephens Green, Dublin opened
       to the public.

1881   Royal University established.
       Coercion Acts.
       Suppression of Land League.

1882   Election of Franklin D. Roosevelt.
       d. of Anthony Trollope, Henry
       Wadsworth Longfellow, Charles
       Darwin, and Ralph Waldo Emerson.

1882   Phoenix Park murders by the
       Invincibles.
       b. of James Joyce, Eamon de
       Valera, and James Stephens.
       University College Dublin
       founded.
1883   Tom Clarke sentenced to penal
       servitude for life.

1884   General C. G. Gordon reaches
       Khartoum.

1884   Gaelic Athletic Association
       founded.

1885   John O'Leary released from
       prison; returns to Dublin.

1887   Queen Victoria celebrates her Golden
       Jubilee.
       Foundation of the Théatre Libre in
       Paris.

1887   National Library of Ireland estab-
       ished.

1890   d. of Cardinal Newman.
       Peak of the Symbolist movement.

1890   Divorce court verdict against
       Charles Stewart Parnell.

163

CHRONOLOGYLITERATURE

Ireland

England, Europe, America, etc.

Sir J. G. Frazer. *The Golden bough.*
William James. *The Principles of psychology.*
Emily Dickinson. *Poems.*
1891 Maurice Barrès. *Le Jardin de Bérénice.*
Thomas Hardy. *Tess of the D'Urbervilles.*
Rudyard Kipling. *The Light that failed.*
G. B. Shaw. *Quintessence of Ibsenism.*
Hamlin Garland. *Main-travelled roads.*

1892 W. B. Yeats. *The Countess Cathleen.*

1892 G. B. Shaw. *Mrs Warren's profession.*
Rudyard Kipling. *Barrack-room ballads.*
Oscar Wilde. *Lady Windermere's fan.*
Henrik Ibsen. *The Master Builder.*
Maurice Maeterlinck. *Pelléas et Mélisande.*
Gerhard Hauptmann. *Die Weber.*
Stephen Crane. *Maggie: a girl of the streets.*

1893 Douglas Hyde. *Love songs of Connacht.*
W. B. Yeats. *The Celtic twilight.*
1894 W. B. Yeats. *Cathleen Ni Houlihan.*
Somerville & Ross. *The Real Charlotte.*
AE. *Homeward: songs by the way.*
1895 *Irish Homestead* begins.

1893 F. H. Bradley. *Appearance and reality.*
Sir Arthur Pinero. *The Second Mrs Tanqu*
Stéphane Mallarmé. *Vers et Prose.*
1894 George Moore. *Esther Waters.*
G. B. Shaw. *Arms and the man.*

1895 Joseph Conrad. *Almayer's folly.*
Stephen Crane. *The Red badge of courage.*
Thomas Hardy. *Jude the obscure.*
The Yellow Book (1895-97).
Oscar Wilde. *The Importance of being Earnest*
1896 Anton Chekhov. *The Seagull.*
Henri Bergson. *Matière et mémoire.*
A. E. Housman. *A Shropshire lad.*

1897 George Sigerson. *Bards of the gael and gall.*
Sir Samuel Ferguson. *Lays of the Red Branch.*
AE. *The Earth breath.*

1898 Émile Zola. *J'accuse.*
Thomas Hardy. *Wessex poems.*
Henry James. *The Turn of the screw.*

England, Europe, America, etc.   **Ireland**

1891 d. of Herman Melville and Arthur
      Rimbaud.

1891 d. of Charles Stewart Parnell.
      Congested Districts Board is es-
      tablished, (1891-1923).

1892 d. of Walt Whitman, Lord Alfred
      Tennyson, and Ernest Renan.

1893 Henry Ford builds his first car.

1893 Gaelic League founded.

1894 d. of Oliver Wendall Holmes.
      Peak of the aesthetic movement
      (1894-95).

1894 Sir Horace Plunkett founds the
      Irish Agricultural Organization
      Society.

1895 End of Chinese-Japanese war.
      Marconi invents radio telegraphy.

1896 b. of Austin Clarke and Liam
      O'Flaherty.

1897 First Oireachtas held in Dublin.

1898 d. of Stéphane Mallarmé and Lewis
      Carroll.

1898 County Councils established.
      Tom Clarke released.

Ireland	England, Europe, America, etc.
	H. G. Wells. *The War of the worlds.* Oscar Wilde. *The Ballad of Reading gaol.* G. B. Shaw. *Anthony and Cleopatra* and *Plays pleasant and unpleasant.*
1899 Douglas Hyde. *A Literary history of Ireland.* Edward Martyn. *The Heather field.* Somerville & Ross. *Some Experiences of an Irish R.M.* W. B. Yeats. *The Wind among the reeds.* First issue of *An Claidheamh Soluis.* Arthur Griffith founds *The United Irishman.*	1899 Henrik Ibsen. *When we dead awaken.* André Gide. *Le Prométhée mal enchaîne.* Thorstein Veblen. *The Theory of the leisure class.*
1900 D. P. Moran begins *The Leader.*	1900 Joseph Conrad. *Lord Jim.* Theodore Dreiser. *Sister Carrie.* Anton Chekhov. *Uncle Vanya.* Sigmund Freud. *The Interpretation of dreams.*
	1901 Thomas Mann. *Buddenbrooks.* August Strindberg. *Dance of death.* Frank Norris. *The Octopus.*
1902 Lady Gregory. *Cuchulain of Muirthemne.*	1902 André Gide. *The Immoralist.* Max Gorki. *Lower depths.* John Masefield. *Salt water ballads.* J. M. Barrie. *The Admirable Crichton.* Anton Chekhov. *Three sisters.* William James. *The Varieties of religious experience.*
1903 George Moore. *The Untilled field.* ✛ W. B. Yeats. *Ideas of good and evil.* James Joyce. First stories in AE.'s *Irish Homestead.*	1903 Samuel Butler. *The Way of all flesh.* Henry James. *The Ambassadors.* George E. Moore. *Principia ethica.*
1904 W. B. Yeats. *In the seven woods; The King's threshold;* and *On Baile's strand.* Padraic Colum. *Wild earth.* Lady Gregory. *Spreading the news;* and *Gods and fighting men.* J. M. Synge. *Riders to the sea.* Arthur Griffith. *The Resurrection of Hungary, a parallel for Ireland.*	1904 Joseph Conrad. *Nostromo.* Henry James. *The Golden bowl.* A. C. Bradley. *The Shakespearean tragedy.* Jack London. *The Sea-wolf.* Anton Chekhov. *The Cherry orchard.* Henry Adams. *Mont-Saint-Michel* and *Chartres.*

England, Europe, America, etc.   Ireland

1899 Outbreak of the Boer War (1899-   1899 Irish Literary Theatre's first pro-
      1902).   duction: Yeats's *Countess Cathleen*
                                                     and Edward Martyn *The Heather
                                                     field.*

1900 d. of Oscar Wilde and Friedrich W.   1900 Arthur Griffith begins Cumann na
      Nietzsche.   nGaedhael.
                                                     b. of Seán O' Faoláin.
                                                     Visit of Queen Victoria.

1901 d. of Queen Victoria; accession of
      Edward VII.
      Edwardian era (1901-1910).
1902 Leon Trotsky escapes to England.   1902 Cuala Press (1902-1946).
      d. of Émile Zola.   Maud Gonne plays Cathleen Ni
                                                     Houlihan.

1903 Flight of the Wright brothers.   1903 b. of Frank O'Connor.
                                                     Wyndham Land Act.
                                                     d. of Walter Osborne, painter
                                                     (1859-1903).
1904 Russo-Japanese war.   1904 Opening of the Abbey Theatre.
      d. of Anton Chekhov.   Ulster Literary Theatre founded.

Ireland	England, Europe, America, etc.
1905 Padraic Colum. *The Land.* George Moore. *The Lake.*	1905 Edith Wharton. *House of mirth.* Rainer Rilke. *Stundenbuch.*
1906 First issue of *Sinn Fein.*	1906 John Galsworthy. *Man of property.* Paul Claudel. *Partage de midi.* Upton Sinclair. *The Jungle.*
1907 John M. Synge. *The Playboy of the western world.*	1907 Joseph Conrad. *The Secret agent.* William James. *Pragmatism.* Henri Bergson. *L'Évolution créatrice.*
1908 W. B. Yeats. *Collected works.* Lady Gregory. *The Workhouse ward.*	1908 Arnold Bennett. *The Old wives' tale.*
1909 Padraic Colum. *Wild earth.* John M. Synge. *Poems and translations.*	1909 Guillaume Apollinaire. *L'Enchanteur pourrissant.* Ezra Pound. *Exultations,* and *Personal.*
1910 Lord Dunsany. *A Dreamer's tales.*	1910 E. M. Forster. *Howard's end.* Paul Claudel. *Cinq grandes odes.*
1911 Kuno Meyer. *Ancient Irish poetry.* St John Ervine. *Mixed marriages.* George Moore. *Hail and Farewell* (1911-14).	1911 Edith Wharton. *Ethan Frome.*
1912 Joseph Campbell. *Poems.* James Stephens. *The Crock of gold.* T. C. Murray. *Maurice Harte.* Seumas O'Sullivan. *Poems.* Forrest Reid. *Following darkness.*	1912 Herbert Grierson's edition of poems of John Donne. Paul Claudel. *L'Annonce faite à Marie.* C. G. Jung. *The Theory of psychoanalysis.* *Poetry:* a magazine of verse. Ezra Pound. *Ripostes.*
1913 AE. *Collected poems.*	1913 Marcel Proust. *Remembrance of things past* (1913-18). D. H. Lawrence. *Sons and lovers.* Willa Cather. *O Pioneers!* Thomas Mann. *Death in Venice.* Marcel Proust. *Du côté de chez Swann.* Miguel de Unamuno. *Del Sentimiento trágico de la vida.* Edmund Husserl. *Phenomenology.*
1914 James Joyce. *Dubliners.* George Fitzmaurice. *Five plays.* W. B. Yeats. *Responsibilities.* Lord Dunsany. *Five plays.*	1914 Rupert Brooke. *1914 and other poems.* Ford Madox Ford. *The Good soldier.* D. H. Lawrence. *The Rainbow.* Virginia Woolf. *The Voyage out.* Robert Frost. *North of Boston.* André Gide. *Les Caves du Vatican.* Vachel Lindsay. *The Congo and other poems.*

England, Europe, America, etc.	Ireland

England, Europe, America, etc.

1905 Albert Einstein formulated theory of relativity.

1906 b. of Samuel Beckett.
d. of Henrik Ibsen.

1907 N. Lenin leaves Russia.

1910 d. of William James.
Accession of George V.

1912 Sinking of the Titanic.

1914 First World War (1914-18).

Ireland

1905 Sinn Fein established.
b. of Brian Coffey, Padraic Fallon, and Patrick Kavanagh.

1907 Tom Clarke returns.
Riots at the Abbey Theatre for Synge's *Playboy*.

1908 National University established.
James Larkin begins Irish Transport and General Workers Union.

1909 d. of John Millington Synge.

1910 James Connolly returns from America.

1912 James Connolly and James Larkin begin the Irish Labour Party.

1913 Irish Citizen Army founded.
Lock-out strike in Dublin.
Irish Volunteers founded.

1914 Larne and Howth gun-running.
John Redmond's Woodenbridge speech.

England, Europe, America, etc.   Ireland

1915 Padraic Pearse's oration at the
      funeral of J. O'Donovan (Rossa).
      Sinking of the *Lusitania;*
      d. of Hugh Lane.

1916 d. of Henry James and Jack London.   1916 Easter Rising.
      Battle of the Somme.   Sir Roger Casement hanged.
                                                   Eamon de Valera elected for Sinn
                                                   Fein.

1917 Russian Revolution.   1917 d. of Nathaniel Hone, painter.
                                                   (1831-1917).

1918 d. of Guillaume Apollinaire.   1918 d. of John Redmond.

1919 Alcock and Brown fly the Atlantic.   1919 Anglo-Irish War (1919-1921).
                                                   First meetings of Dail Eireann.

1921 Truce.

1922 d. of Marcel Proust.   1922 Civil War (1922-1923).
      Mussolini leads fascist march on Rome.   Ratification of the Treaty.

Ireland

Sinclair Lewis. *Babbitt.*
Katherine Mansfield. *The Garden party.*
François Mauriac. *Le Baiser au lépreux.*
Edwin A. Robinson. *Collected poems.*
The Criterion founded.
The Fugitive (1922-25).
I. A. Richards. *The Meaning of meaning.*

1923 *Irish Statesman* founded.
Seán O'Casey. *Shadow of a gunman.*
Liam O'Flaherty. *Thy Neighbour's wife.*
Dublin Magazine begins.

1923 E. E. Cummings. *The Enormous room.*
Elmer Rice. *The Adding machine.*
Wallace Stevens. *Harmonium.*

1924 Liam O'Flaherty. *Spring sowing.*
Seán O'Casey. *Juno and the Paycock.*

1924 E. M. Foster. *Passage to India.*
Thomas Mann. *Der Zauberberg.*
Saint-John Perse. *Anabase.*
T. E. Hulme. *Speculations.*
I. A. Richards. *Principles of Literary Criticism.*
Emily Dickinson. *Selected poems.*
Manifeste du Surréalisme.

1925 Daniel Corkery. *The Hidden Ireland.*
Liam O'Flaherty. *The Informer.*
Somerville & Ross. *The Big house at Inver.*

1925 Virginia Woolf. *Mrs. Dalloway.*
E. E. Cummings. *XLI poems.*
Theodore Dreiser. *An American tragedy.*
F. Scott Fitzgerald. *The Great Gatsby.*
Franz Kafka. *The Trial.*
François Mauriac. *Le Désert de l'amour.*
William Carlos Williams. *In the American grain.*

1926 Seán O'Casey. *The Plough and the stars.*
Séamus Ó Grianna. *Cioth is dealán.*

1926 André Gide. *Les Faux monnayeurs.*
Ernest Hemingway. *The Sun also rises.*
Franz Kafka. *The Castle.*
Ezra Pound. *Personal: the collected poems of Ezra Pound.*

1927 F. R. Higgins. *The Dark breed.*
Austin Clarke. *The Son of learning.*

1927 Jean Cocteau. *Orphée and Oedipe-roi.*
Hermann Hesse. *Steppenwolf.*
Marcel Proust. *À la recherche du temps perdu* (1913-27).
Virginia Woolf. *To the lighthouse.*
Martin Heidegger. *Sein und Zeit.*

England, Europe, America, etc.   **Ireland**

d. of Arthur Griffith, Michael Collins and John Butler Yeats, painter (1939-1922). Maunsell publishing house ceases.

1923 Irish Free State under W. T. Cosgrave (1923-1932). William Butler Yeats receives Nobel Prize. d. of Liam Lynch, Cathal Brugha, and Erskine Childers. Ireland joins the Assembly of the League of Nations.

1924 d. of N. Lenin, Joseph Conrad, Franz Kafka.

1924 *Freeman's Journal* ceases (1763-1924).

1926 General Strike in England

1926 Eamon de Valera establishes Fianna Fail. Radio Eireann begins to broadcast.

1927 Electricity Supply Board established. d. of Kevin O'Higgins. Fianna Fail enters Dail. b. of Richard Murphy.

Ireland

England, Europe, America, etc.

John Livingston Lowes. *The Road to Xanadu.*
E. M. Forster. *Aspects of the novel.*

1928   W. B. Yeats. *The Tower.*
Peadar O'Donnell. *Islanders.*
Abbey Theatre rejects *The Silver tassie.*

1928   Evelyn Waugh. *Decline and fall.*
Aldous Huxley. *Point counter point.*
D. H. Lawrence. *Lady Chatterley's lover.*
C. G. Jung. *Relationships between the ego and the unconscious.*
Vernon L. Parrington. *Main currents in American thought.*

1929   Liam O'Flaherty. *The Mountain tavern.*
Tomás Ó Criomthain. *An t-Oileánach*
Elizabeth Bowen. *The Last September.*
Denis Johnston. *The Old lady says 'no'*
Austin Clarke. *Pilgrimage.*

1929   William Faulkner. *The Sound and the fury.*
Ernest Hemingway. *A Farewell to arms.*
A. N. Whitehead. *The Function of reason.*
I. A. Richards. *Practical criticism.*

1930   W. H. Auden. *Poems.*
Hart Crane. *The Bridge.*
T. S. Eliot. *Ash Wednesday.*
Robert Frost. *Collected poems.*
William Empson. *Seven Types of amgibuity.*
John M. Keynes. *Treatise on money.*

1931   Daniel Corkery. *Synge and Anglo-Irish literature.*
Kate O'Brien. *Without my cloak.*
Frank O'Connor. *Guests of the nation.*
Denis Johnston. *The Moon in the yellow river.*

1931   William Faulkner. *Sanctuary.*
Edmund Wilson. *Axel's castle.*

1932   Austin Clarke. *The Bright temptation.*
Seán O'Faoláin. *Midsummer night madness.*
Liam O'Flaherty. *Skerrett.*
Frank O'Connor. *The Saint and Mary Kate.*
Peadar O'Donnell. *The Gates flew open.*
Francis Stuart. *The Coloured dome.*

1932   William Faulkner. *Light in August.*
Erskine Caldwell. *Tobacco road.*
F. R. Leavis. *New bearings in English poetry.*
Scrutiny (1932-53).

England, Europe, America, etc.   Ireland

1928 Election of Chiang Kai-shek.   1928 Opening of the Gate Theatre.
      d. of Thomas Hardy.   b. of Thomas Kinsella.
                                                d. of Padraic O'Conaire and
                                                Standish O'Grady.

1929 Leon Trotsky expelled from Russia. 1929 Censorship of Publications Act.
      Albert Einstein "Unified field theory".
      Collapse of U.S. Stock Exchange.
      World economic depression.

1930 d. of D. H. Lawrence.

                                          1931 *The Irish Press* begins.
                                                d. of Harry Clarke, painter,
                                                (1889-1931).
                                                d. of William Orphen, painter,
                                                (1878-1931).

                                          1932 Fianna Fail come to power.
                                                Eamon de Valera in office (1932-1948).
                                                Eucharistic Congress in Dublin.

Ireland

England, Europe, America, etc.

1933 Muiris Ó Súileabhain. *Fiche blian ag fás.*

1933 T. S. Eliot. *The Use of poetry and the use of criticism.*
Federico García Lorca. *Blood wedding.*
André Malraux. *La Condition humaine.*
F. R. Leavis and Denys Thompson. *Culture and environment.*
Hart Crane. *Collected poems.*
Stephen Spender. *Poems.*

1934 Seán Ó'Faoláin. *A Nest of simple folk.*
Forrest Reid. *Brian Westby.*

1934 Maud Bodkin. *Archetypal patterns in poetry.*
C. Day Lewis. *A Hope for poetry.*
Ezra Pound. *Make it new.*
John O'Hara. *Appointment in Samarra.*
Malcolm Cowley. *Exile's return.*
John Dewey. *Art as experience.*

1935 T. S. Eliot. *Collected poems; Murder in the cathedral.*
J. T. Farrell. *Studs Lonigan.*
Wallace Stevens. *Ideas of order.*

1936 Austin Clarke. *Collected poems;* and *The Singing men at Cashel.*
Seán O'Faoláin. *Bird alone.*
Francis Stuart. *The White hare.*
Francis Hackett. *The Green lion.*
Peig Sayers. *Peig.*

1936 David Jones. *In parenthesis.*
F. R. Leavis. *Revaluation.*
Dylan Thomas. *Twenty-five poems.*
Georges Bernanos. *The Diary of a country priest.*
John M. Keynes. *General theory of employment, interest and money.*
Anthony O. Lovejoy. *The Great chain of being.*

1937 Liam O'Flaherty. *Famine.*

1937 W. H. Auden. *On this island.*
John Dos Passos. *U. S. A.*
Jean-Paul Sartre. *La Nausée.*
Emily Dickinson. *Collected poems.*

1938 Austin Clarke. *Night and morning.*
Seán O'Faoláin. *King of the beggars.*
Samuel Beckett. *Murphy.*
Patrick Kavanagh. *The Green fool.*

1938 William Carlos Williams. *The Complete collected poems 1906-1935.*
Graham Greene. *Brighton rock.*
Thornton Wilder. *Our town.*
A. N. Whitehead. *Modes of thought.*
George Santayana. *The Realm of truth.*
E. E. Cummings. *Collected poems.*
John Crowe Ransom. *The World's body.*

1939 James Joyce. *Finnegans wake.*
Flann O'Brien. *At swim two birds.*

1939 *Horizon* (1939-50).
Thomas Mann. *Lotte in Weimer.*

England, Europe, America, etc.   **Ireland**

1933 F. D. Roosevelt becomes U.S. President. 1933 d. of George Moore.
Adolf Hitler becomes Chancellor of
Germany.
Famine in Russia.

1935 d. of Lady Gregory and of AE.

1936 d. of Rudyard Kipling.   1936 I.R.A. declared illegal.
Spanish Civil War begins.
F. D. Roosevelt re-elected.
Leon Trotsky exiled.
Accession and abdication of Edward
VIII, accession of George VI.

1937 New constitution.
Douglas Hyde elected first President of Ireland.

1938 The Munich Agreement.   1938 Anglo-Irish Agreement.

1939 World War II (1939-1945).   1939 d. of William Butler Yeats.
d. of Ford Madox Ford.   b. of Seamus Heaney.

Seán O'Casey. *I knock at the door, 1880-1890.*
Michael McLaverty. *Call my brother back.*
Austin Clarke. *Sister Eucharia.*
Louis MacNeice. *Autumn journal.*
1940 *The Bell* begins publication.
Frank O'Connor. *Dutch interior.*
Sean O'Casey. *Purple dust.*

1941 Kate O'Brien. *Land of spices.*
Myles na Gopaleen. *An Béal bocht.*

1942 Mary Lavin. *Tales from Bective Bridge.*
Seán O'Faoláin. *The Great O'Neill.*
Comhar begins publication.

1945 Valentin Iremonger. *Reservations.*

John Steinbeck. *Grapes of wrath.*
Katherine Anne Porter. *Pale horse, pale rider.*
Cleanth Brooks. *Modern poetry and the tradition.*

1940 Graham Greene. *The Power and the glory.*
W. H. Auden. *Another time.*
Richard Wright. *Native son.*
Arthur Koestler. *Darkness at noon.*
Ernest Hemingway. *For whom the bell tolls.*

1941 Bertolt Brecht. *Mutter Courage und ihre kinder.*
Kenneth Burke. *The Philosophy of literary form.*
Reinhold Niebuhr. *The Nature and destiny of man* (1931-43).
Edmund Wilson. *The Wound and the bow.*

1942 Albert Camus. *L'Étranger.*
Jean Anouilh. *Antigone.*
Wallace Stevens. *Notes towards a supreme fiction.*

1943 Thomas Mann. *Joseph and his brethren.*
Jean-Paul Sartre. *L'Être et le néant.*

1944 T. S. Eliot. *Four quartets.*
Jean-Paul Sartre. *No exit.*
Tennessee Williams. *The Glass menagerie.*
Jean Genêt. *Notre Dame des fleurs.*

1945 George Orwell. *Animal farm.*
John Betjeman. *New bats in old belfries.*
Philip Larkin. *The North ship.*
Arthur M. Schlesinger. *The Age of Jackson.*
Evelyn Waugh. *Brideshead revisited.*
W. H. Auden. *Collected poetry.*

England, Europe, America, etc.	Ireland
End of Spanish civil war.	Oireachtais literary competitions re-established.

1940 Leon Trotsky assassinated.
     F. D. Roosevelt re-elected.
     Churchill becomes Prime Minister.
     Dunkirk.
     Battle of Britain.

1940 Lyric Theatre Company founded.
     d. of Roderick O'Connor, painter, (1860-1940).

1941 Manhattan project begins.
     German invasion of Russia.
     Pearl harbour bombed by the Japanese.

1941 d. of James Joyce and F. R. Higgins.

1942 Fall of Singapore.
     General Rommel takes Tobruk.
     Hitler begins extermination of the Jews.

1943 Eighth Army reaches Tripoli.

1943 Sir Basil Brooke becomes Prime Minister of Northern Ireland (1943-1963).
     d. of Sarah Purser, painter, (1849-1943).
     d. of Jerome Connor, sculptor, (1876-1943).

1944 D-Day landings in Normandy.

1944 American troops arrive in Northern Ireland.

1945 Three Power occupation of Berlin.
     Hiroshima and Nagasaki bombed.
     Nuremberg trials begin.
     d. of Paul Valéry, Theodore Dreiser and Franklin D. Roosevelt.

1945 d. of Albert Power, sculptor, (1883-1945).

Ireland	England, Europe, America, etc.

1946 Benedict Kiely. *Land without stars.*
Kate O'Brien. *That lady.*

1946 Dylan Thomas. *Deaths and entrances.*
Simone de Beauvoir. *Tous les hommes sont mortels.*
Eugene O'Neill. *The Iceman cometh.*

1947 Patrick Kavanagh. *A Soul for sale.*
Seán O'Faoláin. *The Irish.*

1947 Albert Camus. *La Peste.*
Robert Lowell. *Lord Weary's castle.*
Cleanth Brooks. *The Well-wrought urn.*

1948 Patrick Kavanagh. *Tarry Flynn.*
Francis Stuart. *A Pillar of cloud.*
Bryan MacMahon. *The Lion-tamer and other stories.*
Michael McLaverty. *The Game cock and other stories.*
Liam O'Flaherty. *Two lovely beasts.*
Feasta begins publication.

1948 W. H. Auden. *Age of anxiety.*
Ezra Pound. *The Pisan cantos.*
A. C. Kinsey. *Sexual behaviour in the human male.*
Robert E. Spiller. *The Literary history of the United States.*
Theodore Roethke. *The Lost son and other poems.*
F. R. Leavis. *The Great tradition.*
Robert Graves. *The White goddess.*

1949 Máirtín Ó Cadhain. *Cré na cille.*
Máirtín Ó Direáin. *Rogha dánta.*

1949 Arthur Miller. *Death of a salesman.*
George Orwell. *Nineteen eighty-four.*

1950 Benedict Kiely. *Modern Irish fiction.*
Seán Ó Tuama. *Nuabhearsaiocht: 1939-1949.*

1950 W. H. Auden. *Collected shorter poems.*
Charles Olson. *Projective verse.*
Ezra Pound. *Seventy cantos.*
Robert Lowell. *Poems 1938-1949.*
Lionel Trilling. *The Liberal imagination.*

1951 Samuel Beckett. *Malone meurt: Molloy.*

1951 W. H. Auden. *Nones.*
Robert Lowell. *The Mills of the Kavanaughs.*
Robert Frost. *Complete poems.*
J. D. Salinger. *Catcher in the rye.*
Tennessee Williams. *The Rose tattoo.*
William Carlos Williams. *Paterson.* Books I-IV, 1946-1951.
Anthony Powell. *A Question of upbringing.*

1952 Frank O'Connor. *The Stories of Frank O'Connor.*
Mervyn Wall. *Leaves for the burning.*
Seán Ó Riordáin. *Eireaball Spideoige.*

1952 Marianne Moore. *Collected poems.*
Dylan Thomas. *Collected poems.*
Evelyn Waugh. *Men at arms.*

1953 Samuel Beckett. *L'Innommable* and *En attendant Godot.*
Liam O'Flaherty. *Dúil.*

1953 Simone de Beauvoir. *The Second sex.*
Donald Davie. *Purity of diction in English verse.*

1954 Kingsley Amis. *Lucky Jim.*
Theodore Roethke. *The Waking: poems 1933-1953.*

England, Europe, America, etc.   Ireland

1946   Isotope Carbon 13 discovered.
       First Assembly of United Nations.

1947   Marshall Plan begins.
       Discovery of the Dead Sea scrolls.

1948   Berlin Airlift begins.

                                                  1949   d. of Douglas Hyde.
                                                         Ireland declared an independent
                                                         Republic.

1950   d. of George Bernard Shaw.
       Korean War begins.

1951   d. of André Gide.   1951   Controversy over Mother and
                                                         Child Scheme.
                                                         John A. Costello's government
                                                         resigns.
                                                         Dolmen Press established.
                                                         Abbey Theatre burns down.

1952   H-Bomb tested in Pacific.
       Accession of Queen Elizabeth II.

1953   d. of Stalin, Dylan Thomas, Eugene   1953   Pike Theatre Club opened.
       O'Neill, and Virginia Woolf.

1954   Algerian War.

		Wallace Stevens. *Collected poems.*
		William Golding. *Lord of the flies.*
		Iris Murdoch. *Under the net.*

1955   Brian Moore. *Judith Hearne.*
James Plunkett. *The Trusting and
the maimed.*
Richard Murphy. *The Archaeology
of love.*

1955   Evelyn Waugh. *Officers and gentlemen.*
Jean Genêt. *The Balcony.*
Philip Larkin. *The Less deceived.*
Robbe-Grillet. *Le Voyeur.*

1956   Brendan Behan. *The Quare fellow.*
Liam O'Flaherty. *The Stories of
Liam O'Flaherty.*

1956   John Osborne. *Look back in anger.*

1957   Seán Ó'Faoláin. *Finest stories.*
Terence de Vere White. *A Fretful
midge.*
Máire Mhac an tSaoi. *Margadh na
saoire.*

1957   William Faulkner. *The Town.*
Jack Kerouac. *On the road.*
John Braine. *Room at the top.*
Gore Vidal. *A Visit to a small
planet.*
Ted Hughes. *The Hawk in the rain.*

1958   Thomas Kinsella. *Another
September.*
John Montague. *Forms of exile.*
T. K. Whitaker. *Economic develop-
ment.*

1958   J. K. Galbraith. *The Affluent society.*
Lawrence Durrell. *Balthazar.*
Harold Pinter. *The Birthday party.*
Robert Penn Warren. *Promises: poems
1954-56.*

1959   Mary Lavin. *Selected stories.*

1959   Robert Lowell. *Life studies.*
Eugene Ionesco. *Les Rhinocéros.*
Günther Grass. *Die Blechtrommel.*
Muriel Spark. *Momento mori.*
Stanley Kunitz. *Selected poems:
1928-1958.*
Pierre Teilhard de Chardin. *The
Phenomenon of man.*

1960   Edna O'Brien. *The Country girls.*
Seán Ó Tuama. *An Grá in amhráin
na ndaoine.*

1960   John Betjeman. *Summoned by bells.*
John Updike. *Rabbit, run.*
Alan Sillitoe. *The Loneliness of the
long distance runner.*
Harold Pinter. *The Caretaker.*
Ted Hughes. *Lupercal.*
Sylvia Plath. *Colossus.*

1961   Austin Clarke. *Later poetry.*

1961   Jean Anouilh. *Becket.*
John Osborne. *Luther.*
Iris Murdoch. *A Severed head.*
Joseph Heller. *Catch 22.*
Thom Gunn. *My sad captains.*

1962   Máirtín Ó Direáin. *Ár ré dhearóil.*
Brian Friel. *The Saucer of larks.*

1962   Alexander Solzhenitsyn. *One day in the
life of Ivan Denisovich.*

England, Europe, America, etc.   **Ireland**

1955 d. of Paul Claudel, Thomas Mann,   1955 Ireland enters United Nations.
      Albert Einstein, and Alexander   d. of Evie Hone (1894-1955),
      Fleming.   stained glass artist.

1956 d. of Bertolt Brecht.   1956 Economic crisis.

1957 U.S.S.R. launches Sputnik I and II. 1957 First Dublin Theatre Festival.
      Desegregation crisis in Little Rock,   Fianna Fail return to power
      Arkansas.   (1957-1963).
                                                The Lantern Theatre opens in
                                                Dublin.
                                                d. of Jack Butler Yeats, painter,
                                                (1871-1957).
                                          1958 First programme for economic
                                                expansion.

                                          1959 Eamon de Valera becomes third
                                                President of Ireland.
                                                d. of Denis Devlin.

1960 John F. Kennedy elected President. 1960 Irish soldiers killed in the Congo.
      d. of Albert Camus.

                                          1961 Ireland enters UNESCO.
                                                Television service begins.

1962 Second Vatican Council held in
      Rome.

Ireland   **England, Europe, America, etc.**

Edward Albee. *Who's afraid of Virginia Woolf.*

James Baldwin. *Another country.*

1963   Richard Murphy. *Sailing to an island.*   1963   Mary McCarthy. *The Group.*

John McGahern. *The Barracks.*   William Carlos Williams. *Pictures from Brueghel.*

John Broderick. *Don Juaneen.*   Charles Tomlinson. *A Peopled landscape.*

1964   Patrick Kavanagh. *Collected poems.*   1964   Peter Weiss. *Marat-Sade.*

Frank O'Connor. *Collection two.*   Philip Larkin. *The Whitsun weddings.*

Denis Devlin. *Collected poems.*

Seán Ó Riordáin. *Brosna.*

John Montague. *Death of a chieftain.*

1965   Robert Lowell. *For the Union dead.*

Sylvia Plath. *Ariel.*

1966   Seamus Heaney. *Death of a naturalist.*   1966   Bernard Malamud. *The Fixer.*

Aidan Higgins. *Langrishe, go down.*   John Barth. *Giles goat-boy.*

Austin Clarke. *Mnemosyne lay in dust.*

Louis MacNeice. *Collected poems.*

Brian Friel. *Philadelphia, here I come!*

John B. Keane. *The Field.*

1967   Flann O'Brien. *The Third policeman.*   1967   Tom Stoppard. *Rosencrantz and Guildenstern are dead.*

John Montague. *A Chosen light.*   Harold Pinter. *The Homecoming.*

Ted Hughes. *Wodwo.*

1968   John Hewitt. *Collected poems.*

Benedict Kiely. *Dogs enjoy the morning.*

Thomas Kinsella. *Nightwalker.*

1969   James Plunkett. *Strumpet city.*   1969   Nathalie Sarraute. *Entre la vie et la mort.*

Richard Power. *The Hungry grass.*   Kurt Vonnegut. *Slaughterhouse five.*

Vladimir Nabokov. *Ada.*

Charles Tomlinson. *The Way of a world.*

1970   *Irish University Review: a journal of Irish Studies* begins publication.   1970   Saul Bellow. *Mr. Sammler's planet.*

Ted Hughes. *Crow: from the life and songs of the crow.*

England, Europe, America, etc.   Ireland

1963 d. of William Carlos Williams and Theodore Roethke. John F. Kennedy assassinated. d. of Sylvia Plath.	1963 Visit of John F. Kennedy. d. of Louis MacNeice.
1964 Vietnam War intensified.	1964 d. of Seán O'Casey, Brendan Behan, and Seán O'Sullivan, painter.
1965 d. of T. S. Eliot.	1965 Seán Lemass exchanges visits with the Northern Ireland Premier, Terence O'Neill. d. of Daniel Corkery.
	1966 New Abbey Theatre opened. d. of Frank O'Connor and Flann O'Brien.
1967 First human heart transplant.	1967 d. of Patrick Kavanagh.
	1968 Demonstrations by Civil Rights Association in Northern Ireland.
	1969 Rioting in Northern Ireland. Samuel Beckett receives Nobel Prize.
	1970 d. of Máirtín O Cadhain.

Ireland

England, Europe, America, etc.

1971 Francis Stuart. *Black List/Section H.*
W. R. Rodgers. *Collected poems.*
Thomas Kilroy. *The Big chapel.*
Mary Lavin. *Collected stories.*

1971 Sylvia Plath. *The Bell jar.*

1972 Thomas Kinsella. *New poems.*
Derek Mahon. *Lives.*
Jennifer Johnston. *The Captains and the kings.*

1972 Donald Davie. *Collected poems 1950-1970.*

1973 John Banville. *Birchwood.*

1973 Kurt Vonnegut. *Breakfast of champions.*
Thomas Pynchon. *Gravity's rainbow.*
Charles Tomlinson. *Written on water.*

1974 Padraic Fallon. *Poems.*
Austin Clarke. *Collected Poems*
Irish University Review: special Austin Clarke issue.
John McGahern. *The Leavetaking.*
Richard Murphy. *High island.*

1975 Julia O'Faolain. *Women in the wall.*
Brian Coffey. *Advent.* In *Irish University Review* special Coffey issue.
Seamus Heaney. *North.*

1976 Denis Johnston. *The Brazen horn.*
Liam O'Flaherty. *The Pedlar's Revenge and Other Stories*
Sean O'Faolain. *Foreign Affairs*
John Banville. *Doctor Copernicus*

England, Europe, America, etc.

Ireland

1971 Internment introduced in Northern Ireland.

1972 Bloody Sunday in Derry.

1973 End of Vietnam War.
d. of Pablo Neruda and W. H. Auden.

1973 Ireland joins the E.E.C.

1974 Worldwide inflation.

1974 d. of Austin Clarke and Padraic Fallon.

1975 d. of Éamon de Valera.

1976 d. of Chairman Mao